THE SOUL OF A BUSINESS

THE SOUL

of a

BUSINESS

MANAGING
FOR PROFIT AND
THE COMMON GOOD

Tom Chappell

BANTAM BOOKS
NEW YORK   TORONTO   LONDON   SYDNEY   AUCKLAND

THE SOUL OF A BUSINESS
A Bantam Book

PUBLISHING HISTORY
Bantam hardcover edition / November 1993
Bantam trade paperback edition / November 1994

ISBN 0-553-37415-X

This book is printed on recycled paper.

Published simultaneously in the United States and Canada

Bantam Books are published by Bantam Books, a division of Bantam Dou-
bleday Dell Publishing Group, Inc. Its trademark, consisting of the words
"Bantam Books" and the portrayal of a rooster, is Registered in U.S. Patent
and Trademark Office and in other countries. Marca Registrada. Bantam
Books, 1540 Broadway, New York, New York 10036.

PRINTED IN THE UNITED STATES OF AMERICA

BVG   0 9 8 7 6 5 4 3 2

To Kate, whose love, creativity, and wisdom have inspired me in an enduring partnership in marriage, parenting, and business,

a n d

to Libby, who envisioned this book and affirmed me with her presence and assurances until I, too, could see. May your spirit, Libby, share in this moment of victory!

S p e c i a l   a p p r e c i a t i o n

to Chris, Matt, Sarah, Eliza, and Luke, my children, who share my hope for a more just world,

a n d

to my mother and father, who by their love and actions taught me religious sensitivity, Yankee ingenuity, and courage.

CONTENTS

INTRODUCTION

T his is not a book about religion and work. It is not about God as CEO, and it is not about New Age spirituality in the workplace. It's about how mind and spirit can work together to compete for profit and market share. It's about how to use the two sides of all of us, the spiritual and the practical, to achieve whatever business goals you set for yourself.

By *spirit* or *spiritual,* I mean the part of you that survives when you eliminate your flesh and bones—the part you can't point to but can feel, the part you might describe to someone else as your essential being, your soul. Soul is what connects you to everyone and everything else. It is the sum of all the choices you make. It is where your beliefs and values reside. Soul is at the center of our relationships to others, and for me it is at the center of the business enterprise.

They don't tell you this in business school or in the Fortune 500. I had to spend four years at the Harvard Divinity School to find out that my religious beliefs, my respect for people and the environment—my *values*—did not have to get in the way of making a profit. I learned that you could, as the Quakers used to say, "do well by doing good." I came to believe this so strongly that I persuaded my board of directors and my managers to make it our company's main "mission" to seek financial success while behaving in a socially responsible and environmentally sensitive way. Not only has my unusual approach to business kept my company competitive, but our success has forced some of the biggest corporations in the nation to follow our lead.

I am an entrepreneur, the president and co-founder with my wife, Kate, of a company called Tom's of Maine. In 1974 we were the first to market a toothpaste made wholly from natural ingredients. Over the next seven years our company put several more products on the shelves aimed at consumers who, like Kate and myself, care about what is actually in the things they buy. We located a new market for personal-care products among the customers of health food stores. By 1981, the company Kate and I had started with a $5,000 loan and a prayer was registering $1.5 million in sales. The prospects for growth were vast, particularly when we decided to sell our natural products in supermarkets and drugstores. A 1986 story on the company's expansion in *The Washington Post* quoted the buyer of a major supermarket chain describing Tom's of Maine as "doing a hell of a job."

I owned a six-bedroom, eighteenth-century Federal-style house on Main Street in a picture-postcard New England town. I had two cars and a forty-foot Hinckley sailing yawl. I had five terrific kids, three of them in boarding school. The woman I loved and respected was not only my wife but my business partner. I had achieved, it seemed, the American dream and then some. But a few years ago I felt that something was missing, something was wrong. I was miserable. In fact, I was more discouraged about what I was doing then than at any other point in my career.

Why was I so unhappy? Because my everyday business life had gone stale. Work had become an unfulfilling exercise. I felt empty, disconnected from my company and my self. I called myself an entrepreneur but I hadn't created a new product in five years. The young professionals I had hired to help me grow my company were taking Tom's of Maine in directions that I was not so sure I wanted it to go. I was still making my numbers, but I was beginning to think twice about the personal and professional meaning of work, money, possessions, power, and prestige. I considered cashing in, selling the company, and retiring at age forty-three.

Instead, after some serious thought and discussions with wise friends, I decided to apply to divinity school. To try to understand my unhappiness, I set out on a search for meaning, a search that grew out of a need to integrate my own spirit with the spirits of my colleagues and co-workers in collective service to our customers. I needed to recapture what had inspired me to start the business in the first place. I needed to get back in touch with my original sense of purpose and to renew myself and my commitment to creating good products. Other entrepreneurs recharge their batteries by working on their golf game or climbing the Matterhorn. I thought I might have better luck reading the great moral and religious thinkers.

Religion has always played an important part in my life. As a boy growing up in western Massachusetts, I sang in the choir and served as an acolyte at the local Episcopal church. In college I added a few religion courses to my English major. When Kate and I moved to Maine in 1968, we joined the Episcopal church in our new town, Kennebunk. But no one in the parish would have mistaken me for a religious nut or even a future divinity school student. Religion had by no means dominated my life, but I did seem to have this nagging urge to know more about how my life fit into God's plan, what greater meaning my life's work had.

I assured the board of directors that I was not intending to drop out of the business entirely. My plan was to pursue a master's degree in theology at the Harvard Divinity School, only a ninety-minute drive away in Cambridge, two days a week. The rest of the time I would still be CEO of Tom's of Maine. If a few of the board members thought I had flipped, their fears were assuaged by others who approved of my decision. (Doubtless some of the board members figured my absence would allow the young wizards we hired to go about their business expanding Tom's of Maine, spared the glare of Tom.)

So twenty years after I had graduated from college, I went back to school, juggling my studies with my duties as husband, father, manager, and confused leader of a then–$5 million American company. As I sat in the lecture halls and seminar rooms of the Harvard Divinity School, one question seemed to focus my thoughts: Could I stick to my respect for humanity and nature and still make a successful company even more successful? I found my answers in the writings of the great philosophers, Immanuel Kant, Jonathan Edwards, and Martin Buber, who clarified for me that, You don't have to sell your soul to make your numbers. Nor do you have to give up good sound business practices to allow your values to participate in even the smallest, most pragmatic business transactions. Suddenly, I entertained the possibility that I could actually find a way to manage for profit *and* for the common good.

Even more amazing—and gratifying—I discovered during those four years in divinity school that the intuitions with which Kate and I had started out had been on the mark. We had always believed that we ought to treat our customers as if they were ourselves, that a company that cared about its products and put the customer first would make money. We had built a company whose strength is rooted in our disposition to care about our customers and in our willingness to risk letting our values inform our competitive strategy.

But back in the 1970s that was just a feeling Kate and I had had, a feeling that seemed to run counter to all the best professional advice we could buy about how to grow our company. My studies at Harvard confirmed for me that Kate and I had been right and the bean-counters wrong—at least about Tom's of Maine. My professional life had turned sour amid Tom's of Maine's amazing success because I had allowed the company to swerve away from Kate's and my instincts about what kind of company we wanted to run. Trying to manage a successful, growing company, I had forgotten what had made me a business success in the first place: going with my gut, risking the farm, chasing my visions rather than stopping to analyze every single trend to death—being an *entrepreneur.*

Is there an entrepreneur who ever scored big by ignoring his gut? Typically, entrepreneurs succeed by *bucking* the conventional wisdom. Entrepreneurs create new markets out of nothing more than their vision or their imagination. How do they know the market is there? Well, they just *see* it, very, very clearly, and they just *feel* it, very, very intensely.

Like Mo Siegel, the co-founder of Celestial Seasonings, the tea company. In the natural-ingredients business—my business—the most successful entrepreneurs have been those who looked at our culture's crazy habits and purchase patterns and wondered how in the world we got so caught up in buying things that are so unhealthy. Siegel asked why we drink so much tea and coffee when we know caffeine is harmful to our health. He proved that herbal teas are not only healthy and tasty but profitable. Paul Hawken of Erewhon Trading Company and Frank Ford of Arrowhead Mills asked why we have a national diet of rice and grains whose nutritional value is stripped away in processing. They created whole-grain breads and flours and brown rice, thus giving birth to a new way of healthy eating. Ben and Jerry asked why American ice cream has become a frozen swirl of plasticizers, dyes, and artificial flavors whose only connection to a dairy is the farm or cow pictured on the cardboard container. By simply making ice cream the old-fashioned way, with real dairy ingredients, Ben and Jerry became legends in their own time.

In 1974, Kate and I wondered why all toothpastes were full of complex abrasives, dyes, artificial flavors, preservatives, binders, fluoride, and worst of all saccharin, long suspected as a cause of cancer. Why were Americans consuming seven hundred million tubes of toothpaste and spending more than a billion dollars filling their mouths every day with chemicals? Had anyone ever asked if that was what people really wanted in a toothpaste? Kate and I asked—and we've ended up attracting eight million toothpaste buyers and users in America to Tom's of Maine's natural brand. We simply followed our intuitions.

But by the mid-1980s, what had started as an *anti*business business was becoming a big business. Decisions at Tom's of Maine were no longer made by gut instinct; they had become rational calculations. Instead of envisioning the future, we were analyzing the past, like every Fortune 500 company. I myself was split down the middle between entrepreneur and professional manager.

This book is the story of how I rediscovered my values and set out to redirect myself and my company, how I retrieved my entrepreneurial self and acquired a new business vision and new business tools. In my studies at Harvard I learned that many religions view the good life as a balancing act between the spiritual and the practical, the divine and the everyday. All philosophies recognize how difficult it is to maintain spiritual values day in and day out without compromising ourselves. For centuries, Christian mystics and saints have written about finding the *via media*—the middle way. The Hebrew prophets often spoke of finding "the good way" in the world and walking along it. The wisdom of Mahayana Buddhism considers both sides of business conflicts and charts a course down "the Middle Way," between wisdom and compassion.

I think I've found the middle way for Tom's of Maine, where we use our head and heart in planning business strategies. We make room for spirit in the world of commerce. We have two aims, one that serves the individual and one that serves the common good. After reading this book, you can decide whether you, too, can use these tools to take your company down this middle road.

My message is simple: Beliefs drive strategy. Your ethics *can* form the foundation of smart analysis and clear thinking. Your personal values *can* be integrated with managing for all the traditional goals of business—making money, expanded market share, increased profits, retained earnings, and sales growth. Not only can your personal beliefs be brought to work, they can work for you. You can be a hard-assed competitor *and* still run a business with soul.

I also want to prove to you that this Middle Way of doing business can benefit your employees and your community. Ours is an age full of cynicism toward business and its leaders. The fast-moving world of mergers and acquisitions and hostile takeovers has eroded the trust between employers and their employees. But most people want to come to work and do a good job. They want to contribute to the growth and development of a company whose values they believe in. If the company has no principles other than maximizing profit, or if its values are unstated, workers will limit themselves to the least creative principle in business: Please the boss. No wonder we lament the disappearance of creativity among our workers.

A company will thrive when its managers and their employees are in sync. Common values, a shared sense of purpose, can turn a company into a community where daily work takes on a deeper meaning and satisfaction. In this book I will show you how we at Tom's of Maine have tried to build into our decision-making process values that our management and staff hold in common. Like any business, we have our dilemmas; but unlike most businesses, we find answers by drawing on a vision that the entire company agrees upon, from the president to those who unload the trucks: Work hard to make good products for customers who care as much as we do about our health, the environment, and the future of our communities.

What about profit? Don't get me wrong—I'm in business to make money. But that's not my only goal. I believe that the conventional, sole focus of maximizing gains for shareholders strips away that part of ourselves that needs to thrive. Something in us wants to endure beyond retained earnings, and that something is our soul. In this book I will show how Tom's of Maine fits its commitment to the common good into its business strategy without undermining profits. If you nurture the soul of your business, not only can you compete with the biggest players in the game, you will add meaning to your work and make a real contribution to society.

Too many companies view their donations to community projects as mere public relations. At Tom's of Maine doing good is at the center of the business enterprise. Doing good is, in fact, the reason we're doing so well. Dedicating a percentage of profits to support the arts, education, the environment, and human needs is a *gain* for any business strategy, not a cost. Setting out to be the lowest-cost producer is meaningful only if you also set out to be the highest-quality giver; today's discerning consumers demand both. We expect priests and teachers, artists and naturalists, to care for and celebrate the human spirit. Shouldn't we expect the same from CEOs?

At a recent board meeting, one member—the dean of one of the nation's leading business schools—joked that our 31 percent growth in sales in that fiscal year, along with our 41 percent increase in profits, had been surpassed only by our spiritual growth of 50 percent. In this comment lies a serious challenge to the practice of business as usual in America: If integrating a sense of the common good into their business strategy can actually help companies increase profits, what excuse can they make for moving forward unconcerned about their communities, the environment, and the future? Tom's of Maine is hardly unique. We've simply tried to live our values in the marketplace, and it's working. Why can't it work for you? I believe passionately that doing business for the common good can be the mission of any company.

That's why I wrote a book about how one entrepreneur set out on a search for his own soul and found the soul of his business.

I

IDENTITY

IDENTIFYING

VALUES

In 1982, as Tom's of Maine was poised to move from the shelves of health food stores into the wide aisles of major supermarket and drugstore chains, I was sitting in a strategy meeting with my marketing department. The company was about to make the most daring move in its thirteen-year history, and my management team understandably wanted to make our shift into the big time as sure a thing as possible. Marketing proceeded to ask the question that my board had also raised, that market researchers had asked me, and that even people on the street put to me: "Can't Tom's of Maine natural toothpaste get beyond that flavor problem?"

It was a problem, no doubt about it. The main ingredient of our toothpaste—calcium carbonate—leaves a chalky aftertaste. Every other nationally advertised brand adds saccharin to their toothpaste on the presumption that Americans can't apply brush to teeth without something sweet in between. "Would we really lose anything by using sweeteners?" asked the marketing department, eager to yield nothing to the competition.

The question has always ticked me off, and the reason is that it indicates a lack of understanding of our very identity as a company. Tom's of Maine manufactures *natural* products; saccharin is not only artificial, it is a suspected cause of cancer. To add it, no matter what the competitive advantages, would go against everything Tom's of Maine stood for. My position on artificial sweeteners is firm and nonnegotiable. "We've never done it," I said. "We never will. It's not us. That's playing with the product, and we're keeping this formula clean and original."

In elite business schools and large corporations, one idea is hammered into professional managers: Know thy market. But Kate and I had built our little company on the basis of a much older imperative: Know thyself. When we moved to Maine to find a better life for ourselves and our young family, we wanted to use natural products. Few were available, so we decided to create and manufacture our own brand—for us and people like us. Over the next ten years the company we created, which was named Tom's of Maine in 1981, grew to $1.5 million in sales. Thousands of Americans were buying our natural *unsweetened* toothpaste.

Our move into supermarkets and drugstore chains—*without* changing our formula—turned out to be a big success. Between 1981 and 1986, Tom's of Maine jumped to $5 million in sales—an average annual growth rate of 25 percent. It was hard work, and it was emotionally wrenching. To hire the professional talent who knew how to crack the mass market, I had to let go executives who had helped make the company successful in the first place. I spent three days a week in an airplane, flying around the country to meet existing accounts as well as the new ones. I went no place without sales and profit-loss forecasts, financial statements, media strategy, advertising copy, unit sales, and résumés of new hires in my briefcase. I redid budgets on the wing. It was numbers, numbers, numbers.

During this expansion, Tom's of Maine became a very different company from the one Kate and I had started. The company's identity changed in ways we had not intended. Even though we had built a company by dreaming up new products, we had created only one new product in five years. The creative energy of the business had clearly shifted into the diverse analytical tasks that now filled our days—new account development, new market development, new advertising campaigns, financial planning, financial control, management reorganization and evaluations, and new equipment. Tom's had become more successful because it had become more focused and analytical in its business strategy. And the young MBAs and alumni of the big packaged goods companies I had hired (and who had wanted to sweeten our product) had helped make that success possible.

While I wanted Tom's of Maine to continue to be successful, I was not fully satisfied with its success. My new management team wanted to keep growing the company, as did I. But I would not allow us to grow by forgetting the company's commitment to natural ingredients and its customers, to its employees, and to the environment. For five years I waged a constant tug-of-war between my vision of what the company ought to be and my management's. It was hard to argue with their numbers. But something was missing, something was wrong, and I was determined to find what it was. I was even considering selling and quitting Tom's of Maine, a company that had been my whole life for the previous fifteen years.

ORIGINAL VALUES

AND THE FALL

A decade before, the company had been all I cared about. I'd been a man with a mission. Some mornings I would get up and tell Kate that I pitied the poor people I was selling our products to that day; they didn't have a chance of resisting a man who believed so much in what he was doing! I was an entrepreneur who had succeeded in putting one new product after another on the shelves. Between 1971 and 1981, Kate and I had created the first nonpolluting liquid.laundry detergent and the first toothpaste made from natural ingredients. We also invented natural liquid soaps, shampoos, hair rinses, mouthwash, flossing ribbon, shaving creams, bar soaps, and skin lotion. Not all these products were perfect, of course; we decided to discontinue some and concentrate on others.

But Kate and I had taken the business from zip to $1.5 million in sales on our own. We saw ourselves as classic entrepreneurs with no business school degrees, no experience in any giant consumer packaged-goods companies. We had ideas and made them happen. It was in our blood. My father was an entrepreneur; Kate's family had built a silk dynasty in New England. I had been an English major, but I was a born salesman; Kate was a young mother, but she was also a great gardener and cook, skilled at mixing herbs and oils into soap products and able to write ad copy on the side. We were partners, and along with my brother-in-law as plant manager, a former stockbroker as sales manager, and an environmentalist as another plant manager, we had created a successful business.

But with the recession of the late 1970s, the traffic in health food stores was declining, and the growth rate of our brand had slowed. We had three choices: (1) to stay in the health food stores, branching out into skin care and vitamins; (2) to expand into the major supermarket and drugstore chains like Stop & Shop, Pathmark, and CVS/People's; or (3) to sell the company. I was all for option 2—I dreamed of making Tom's of Maine the leader in natural personal-care products in stores selling toothpaste, deodorant, and shampoo nationwide. But my existing team was in no way prepared to achieve such a dream; we knew nothing about the strategies it would take to crack the mass market. One adviser warned us to stay out of the way of Procter & Gamble. "You'll get killed," he said.

I disagreed. But to grow the business, the extended family that we called Tom's of Maine would have to "professionalize." I needed board members with business expertise. I found them: a business school dean signed on, and so did a top New York consultant to a consumer packaged-goods firm who summered in the area and a psychologist who specialized in "organizational development." The new board and I shared a common goal: to expand beyond health food stores where shoppers are health-*committed* to the big supermarkets and drugstore chains where many customers are health-*concerned*. Our strategy called for aggressive growth and profits.

We had to put on a new face, create a new identity to impress the managers of the big supermarkets and drugstore chains. I began an expensive executive search for people with sales and marketing experience in the biggest consumer packaged-goods companies in the nation. After signing two young pros, one from Procter & Gamble, the other from General Mills, who wanted to work for a small business they believed in and raise their families in a beautiful part of the country, Tom's of Maine made its move.

We spent money on a test market in Boston and Portland to learn more about the differences between health-food-store customers and those who shopped in the large supermarket chains and drugstore outlets. We put cash into market research to change our packaging. For health-food-store shoppers, the word *natural* on a tube of toothpaste is redundant; everything in the store is natural. But for a supermarket, where the shelves are lined with a vast array of toothpaste brands, we had to alert the health- and environment-conscious customer to our product by renaming it Tom's of Maine's Natural Toothpaste. We upped our advertising budget—for radio, not television—choosing small markets so that we could quickly gauge the results of our changes.

The new marketing and advertising techniques worked. In Boston alone in two years, we went from a market share of two-tenths of one percent to *two percent*. Within five years, Tom's of Maine had grown from $1.5 million in sales to close to $5 million. My marketing and sales experts had known what they were doing. Whether it had been the *right* thing to do for Tom's was another matter.

This was the issue that I fought over with my young MBAs—and my own instincts. They had helped me get what I wanted, a successful growing company. But I had a feeling that there was more in life than a big business, a big house, and a big boat.

That's why I went to see the Reverend Mr. Malcolm Eckel, a clergyman who had known me all my life.

BREAKING AWAY

In the fall of 1986, I confided to Reverend Eckel at his home, "I'm tired of creating new brands and making money."

I surprised myself with that admission. I had never thought that such a sentence would come out of *me*. But there I was, asserting that though I was very successful, I felt empty. "I'm really not too happy," I said.

Reverend Eckel had known me when I was a boy in his church in the Massachusetts town where I grew up. Now he and his wife, Connie, were retired and living nearby Kennebunk, where Tom's of Maine is headquartered. Malcolm had been a banker before he entered the Church and was therefore just the sort of friend I needed to talk to. I confessed how confused I was about what I should be doing with the rest of my life. I had made a real go of something I'd started. What more could I do in life except make more money? Where was the purpose and direction for the rest of my life? "I think that I would like to study more about theology," I explained. "I'm not really understanding my mission in life."

He cautioned me about making any rash decisions. "Putting on a collar is not always the best solution in the world," he said. I told him I had to try something, and my thoughts kept coming back to the study of theology. Connie, who was preparing lunch and listening, finally interrupted us to ask, "How do you know that Tom's of Maine isn't your ministry?" In other words, maybe my business *was* my mission in life.

It was not a question that I had expected, nor one that I wanted to hear. Fifteen years of Tom's of Maine was the reason I was confused about my life and was searching for some new direction. The idea of finding—through my *business*—a higher mission than making money was not the clean, crisp solution I had thought I was looking for. In hindsight, it probably shows how much I'd been seduced by the absolute nature of the numbers games I'd been playing for five years. I couldn't then envision merging my desire to do something meaningful with the day-to-day nature of business. How could my internal struggles possibly influence my business struggles in any positive way?

I discussed my dilemma with other friends and learned about something called Theological Day, a kind of visitor's day at the Harvard Divinity School. Intrigued, I drove down to Cambridge to check it out. I was attracted by Harvard's nondenominational approach to religious studies, and by the time I returned to Kennebunk, my mind was made up: I wanted to apply.

But first I had to discuss my decision with the Tom's of Maine board and with Kate—especially Kate, who would have to make sacrifices at work and home if I were to go to graduate school. My plan was to split my time between Cambridge and Tom's of Maine. Kate gave me her unequivocal support. The other board members, however, were more ambivalent, skeptical about how my studies could benefit the company, especially at a time when our goal was to increase the growth of Tom's of Maine by about 25 percent a year. Could that happen without Tom on the job full time? While one board member thought my absence might give top management the extra freedom to become more creative, most of the others saw my disappearance, even if only for two days a week, as a detriment. They were kind enough, however, to recognize that the mere prospect of this change had reinvigorated me, and they decided that I was not to be denied my opportunity to be a part-time CEO/theology student for at least a semester. At that point there was still the possibility that Harvard would be no more excited about my application than the Tom's of Maine board.

But the Harvard Divinity School decided to take a chance on a gray-haired entrepreneur, and the following September I was back in Cambridge. Though I still spent two and a half days in Kennebunk running Tom's of Maine, the feeling of freedom from the day-to-day number-crunching grind of business unexpectedly energized and pointed me in new professional directions. Studying theology turned out to be the best business decision I'd ever made.

TOM OF MAINE
MEETS THE WORLD OF IDEAS

During my first few weeks at Harvard, I was a sponge, soaking up ideas and new experiences. I knew this was exactly where I wanted to be, learning about ideas, about myself, and amazingly, about my business. I realized that maybe Harvard would be not a retreat from my business self but its salvation. I had sought refuge in divinity school because I believed that the expansion of Tom's of Maine had split me in two, the idealistic entrepreneur versus the manager of a highly professional, successful, growth-oriented, bottom-line-focused business. After a short time at Harvard, I detected the possibility that I might be able to merge my two sides once again into one happy (business)man.

I was able to translate the philosophical ideas I encountered into business scenarios and apply them to Tom's of Maine almost immediately. In my introductory ethics class with the moral philosopher Arthur Dyck, for instance, I learned that there are different value systems according to which we make moral decisions. Hell, I hadn't even known there was more than one, let alone several. Professor Dyck discussed utilitarianism, the moral view that a good course of action is calculated on the scale of what gives the greatest number of people the most pleasure or the greatest happiness. Contrasting with the utilitarian take on morality is another: choosing what to do on the basis of whether a particular action respects the dignity of others. In the eyes of the utilitarian, the good person is basically a calculating machine that asks: What gives the most pleasure to the most people? The most happiness?

Although the term *utilitarianism* was new to me, I ran into the concept every day in business, where the standard of "good" or "happiness" is what creates *the most profit*. Traditionally in the business world, "the right move" is weighed only according to how profitable it is. If using cheaper materials increases profit, if laying off loyal, hard-working employees increases profit, if polluting the air and rivers increases profit, then so be it. Perhaps I'm judging business motives unfairly, especially in those cases where certain companies do try to provide customers with quality services, but it does seem that by today's norm, "profit is king."

Running a business by the numbers—by *utility*—was precisely what Kate and I had tried to avoid from the beginning. Dyck's class helped me realize that our way of doing business corresponded more to what Dyck calls *formalism*—that inner sense of obligation and human connection that people feel for their friends, neighbors, and family. Kate and I acted out of recognition of these human bonds. We did not believe that making money is the only goal of either business or work. Is an employee happy only if he has more money in his pay envelope? We saw every day that making good products and working in a pleasant environment contributes to happiness in the workplace. In our experience, as much as people want to make more money, they also want to be respected by their bosses and the people they work with. Our relation to our customers was one of respect. Our first customers had been our family and friends. We were not in business to maximize profits by cheating our customers or skimping on quality.

Up until now, it had been hard to argue with the success of our numbers. But for the first time in my career I had the language I needed to debate my bean-counters. I could now begin to bring a fuller perspective of business to them.

I wanted the managers of my company to know that there are alternatives to plotting business strategy according only to how much profit will result. In a planned discussion I set up about the implications of these different ethical systems in the day-to-day life of Tom's of Maine, my chief financial officer and I eventually agreed that people have to be *useful* in producing products, sales, and profits, but they also need to be respected, and that includes sharing in the company's success.

The immediate result of this first attempt to apply our *personal* beliefs and business values to business strategy was our identification of "respect for others" as a *company* value. Our examination of our own identities changed the way we looked not only at ourselves and our colleagues but at our company. To reflect this change in company identity in practical ways—and not just in good feelings—we sought to establish a retirement and profit-sharing plan for employees.

This was only the first small step in an ongoing reevaluation of our internal and external business policies, attitudes, and activities. But it signaled the beginning of a new era at Tom's. More radical revelations and changes were just around the corner.

A BIG LIGHT GOES ON

During one of my days back in the office, I met with my marketing staff about using direct marketing research. Examining examples of the kind of research we might do, I was struck by how detached and judgmental the descriptions of each consumer type were. Affluent people were divided up into categories such as "Gold Coast" and "blue bloods" and "greenbacks" and "Volvo drivers." There were marketing strategies for "survivalists" (that is, people living on food stamps), for wives between eighteen and thirty-five, and for men eighteen to forty-nine. It seemed to me that we were talking about objects here, not human beings. The research, I recognized, grouped people according to their—the terms of Dyck's ethics course seemed so on the mark—"utility." I now realized that this numbers-oriented approach annoyed me because it clashed with my own values, which were based on respecting people as people, not on calculating their utility in machinelike terms.

A few days later, I was back at the divinity school in a class on religious experience taught by Richard Niebuhr, Hollis Professor of Divinity at Harvard. He had asked us to read the twentieth-century religious classic *I and Thou* by the Jewish philosopher Martin Buber. "To man the world is twofold in accordance with his twofold attitude," Buber began his book. In one attitude toward the world, we expect something back from all the relationships we have. We organize, use, abuse, control, and dominate everything—and everybody—in our lives because we want something from these relationships. Buber described this mindset as an "I-It" relation when we treat even other people as objects. The other attitude we can have, however, is our relation to another human *not* for anything in return but in simple respect, love, friendship, and honor for their own sake. Buber called this an "I-Thou" relationship. For Buber, either we live in relationship to the world as an object, something for us to experience or use, or else we love and honor it for its own sake. "In the beginning," wrote Buber, "there is relation."

I remember that day so clearly: sitting in a big lecture hall with fifty or so other students, Niebuhr finishing up, the other students filing out for their next class, Niebuhr himself going through his usual post-lecture ritual of exchanging his reading glasses for another pair, gathering his papers slowly and methodically, and stuffing them into his briefcase, while I remained in my chair, quite stunned at what I had heard and its implications for my life and career. "I-Thou" versus "I-It" relationships. People versus things. The dignity of persons versus their utility. Kate's and my way of doing business versus the methods of professional managers. We had divided the world into two—on Sunday, we indulged in an "I-Thou" relation with God, but during the week it was all "I-It." Buber believed that both relations ought to be integrated into our lives, that to be fully human we can approach the world from the mind and from the spirit. We can respect what we also use.

I finally pulled myself up to approach Niebuhr, a kind and patient man in his sixties who simply listened to this strange student. "This is so powerful. So simple. It's what's wrong with the world," I said. "It's what's wrong with business. Business is all about 'I-It' relationships. Making objects out of people. Making objects out of perceptions and turning them into some kind of useful means-ends activity." Niebuhr nodded, and smiled warmly; this was hardly news to him. But after he left the room, my mind was still racing. Buber had described *my* way of doing business. Kate and I had built Tom's around treating our customers as real people with family histories and futures, not as abstract categories or statistics. I had no interest in using people to maximize our gain; I didn't want to fit them into some inhuman category of marketing research. What we had always cared most about—it had been the center of our business strategy, such as it was, from the beginning—was respecting the human dignity of our customers.

Kate and I had always tried to imagine the customer as someone we could actually talk to face to face. From our first toothpaste package, we had communicated with customers in a letter on the label, informing them about the source and purpose of our ingredients (for example, saying we use fluoride in toothpaste that is found in the sea and prevents cavities), ending with the invitation: "Please write and let us know your experience. Your friends, Tom and Kate."

Thus, instinctively, Kate and I had created an "I-Thou" relationship with our customers. We talked to them, and they had responded. Had they ever! Immediately, we got letters from enthusiastic customers. This kind of one-on-one relationship had nothing to do with the kind of car they drove or their income level. Our customers cared about what was in their products, and they were buying our products because we did too. For Kate and me, this was what business was about.

But when I had expressed such sentiments to other business executives, they would roll their eyes. I remember one evening at our house in Kennebunk, when a visitor, a professional marketing executive, took one look at a bottle of our apple shampoo and exclaimed to everyone within hearing, "I don't see what this product is for! I don't see the product benefits!"

His ridicule of our packaging was a classic "I-It" approach. We didn't claim on the package that our new apple shampoo made your hair shiny and smell like apples. Nor did we imply in our advertising that our shampoo would make your hair as lush and strong as Rapunzel's. Our customers didn't give a damn about such secondary "product benefits." As long as the shampoo cleaned their hair, what they really cared about was what was in the stuff. We told *that* story on the package.

Traditional businessmen just didn't seem to get what Tom's of Maine was doing. But to be fair, at the time I wasn't quite sure what we were up to either. Buber was a revelation. You had to treat a person—

the consumer—as *more* than an object or a statistic. Kate and I had treated our customers as friends or neighbors. It had been easy for us. After all, we had created our company to make the sort of natural products we wanted for our own family but couldn't find; in a very real sense we *were* our customers. Yet it was only at Harvard Divinity that I began to find some business justification for what Kate and I had been doing instinctively with our company all along—creating an "I-Thou" relationship between Tom's of Maine and our customers, and between us and our employees.

I was beginning to re-vision the aims and identity of my company. Jonathan Edwards, a legendary fire-breathing preacher of colonial America, showed me how to translate this vision into reality and create a new way of doing business for Tom's of Maine.

"BEING IS RELATION": A NEW BUSINESS ATTITUDE

Before I went to divinity school, I prided myself on my individualism. New England Yankees like my father and I were self-reliant individuals; we knew how to go it alone. We valued independence and freedom. I remember the emotional high I had felt when incorporating Tom's of Maine. The company was a new, separate entity, and it was mine. America's free-market, self-reliant society had led me to understand the self as something private and separate, similar to a business entity—standing on its own, alone, unencumbered by the expectations of others.

But at Harvard I encountered the writings of Jonathan Edwards, perhaps the most gifted philosopher in the New England colonies if not in American history. Edwards had a radically different notion about identity. "One alone is nothing," wrote Edwards. Over a century before Buber wrote *I and Thou*, Edwards had asked whether our sense of identity comes from being separate, from being individual, distinct from others, or from being *connected* to others. His answer: "Being is nothing but proportion." In other words, a sense of being comes not from unconnected individuality but from a sense of relation to others. We are all individuals, to be sure, but we are not only individuals. Our identity is also shaped by other minds and spirits.

Edwards's version of identity hit me square in the face. I tried to think of myself as wholly separate and distinct, but my mind was unable to empty itself of other references; I couldn't strip my self down to only me. I could think of myself only in relation to others— to God, to Kate, to the rest of my family, to my colleagues, to the company, to the community, and on and on, into what seemed a countless series of interrelations. I had always assumed that the very definition of an *individual* was something separate and distinct from the group.

Many of my fellow students had difficulty with this notion of "being as relation." They felt that it denied them their own individuality. As the classroom debate swirled around these ideas, I heard echoes of all those discussions we had had at Tom's of Maine about our corporate identity, particularly as we sought to move from being a health-food-store supplier into the mass marketplace: Is free enterprise governed by a rule of privacy, and is self-interest designed to maximize shareholder gains? Or is a company only one part of the whole, accountable to society?

From my own personal and professional perspective, I could see that I was a combination of both, an individual but one who had a role to play in the larger scheme of things—an entrepreneur rather than a CEO of a Fortune 500, a capitalist but also a moralist. I recognized that, yes, we are individuals, but each of us also plays a role connected to something more than ourselves, connected by our relations to others, unique but still interdependent.

I now found myself thinking about Tom's of Maine in light of Jonathan Edwards, about my company not only as a private entity but in relation to many other entities—employees, financial partners, customers, suppliers, even the earth itself. Living in a community, we are relational, and we have obligations that go along with those relationships. I thought about the nature of these obligations long and hard. I even scribbled down a diagram of how my own company interrelated with other groups:

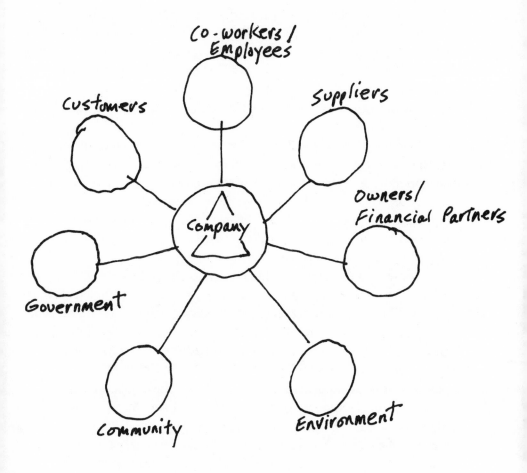

Some of these relationships are obvious to any businessman. A company deals with its suppliers and has an obligation to be clear about what it wants and prompt about paying for what it gets. A business ought to deliver quality and innovation to its customers; for its owners, it has an obligation to build value and pay out dividends. Less obvious, though, is a company's relationship to the environment and the community it lives and does business in. It owes them too. We have no right to foul the air or the waters. The community provides us with services, workers, and profits. We have a responsibility to give something back to them.

In these relationships I began to see the basis for a new approach to a business plan. Tom's of Maine was part of a web of social relationships that called for responsible action. While our *legal* rights protected our privacy, our *moral* obligations force us to reach outside the company. All the obligations I had identified had very tangible definitions, and each represented time and money and priorities we could set.

Jonathan Edwards taught me that what I was—my identity—depended on my relations to others. Buber had told me that for that relation to be genuine, it had to be person-to-person, give-and-take, respectful. This unlikely pair of religious thinkers, a thoroughly Puritan divine from colonial New England and a twentieth-century Jew who had lived in Israel, had refocused my own identity back toward the company I helped create.

I now began to understand that the tensions at Tom's of Maine between me and my young MBAs were a symptom of our different visions of business, of our clash of values. No matter how much those young professionals wanted to work at Tom's of Maine and be "different" from their fellow business school graduates, they had been trained in the same way, indoctrinated into the same business principles, taught to ask the same questions: What will the numbers be this time next year? How do we get the numbers we want? To make those numbers, to get more market share from our competitors, to give us that edge on crowded supermarket shelves, they were more inclined than I to change, even if ever so slightly, those things that made us different.

For more than a decade I had known that my customers care about two things: What is in the product? and Is it good for me? Trained marketers want a "benefit statement" on the package, but for our customers the benefit is the *natural* product.

Only a year before, I hadn't had the intellectual confidence to question the standard ways of doing business. I knew that their way wasn't my way, but what I didn't know was that my way, intuitive though it was, has a firm grounding in Western religious and moral thought. I learned that I wasn't alone—far from it. At Harvard I picked up formidable allies such as Martin Buber and

Jonathan Edwards. I now knew that the "professionals" had a lot to learn from me.

It was a wonderful feeling of rediscovery. The confusion that had accompanied me to Reverend Eckel's house a year and a half before had been replaced by a whole new vision. I had gone to divinity school in search of who I was and what my role was, and I had rediscovered not only what kind of entrepreneur I was (and wanted to be) but the language with which to share it with others. I had become a man with a new mission—namely, to transform Tom's of Maine into a company that continued to live the values that made it successful— selling products that were natural, healthy, and sensitive to the needs of our employees, our customers, and the environment.

There was an alternative to American business as usual, and with the help of Richard Niebuhr and Arthur Dyck—intellectuals who probably hadn't spent a minute thinking about "market share" or "PBT" (Profit Before Taxes)—I finally realized that there was more to my business—to any business—than the numbers. There was its soul.

FORGING

THE MISSION

About the time I began divinity school, I was battling with my top managers over launching a new product. Kate and I had designed a new baking soda toothpaste. Frankly, it tasted like hell, and my head of marketing said, "In all candor, I don't know how we're going to sell it." Kate tried to split the ingredients, using half baking soda and half calcium carbonate, the main teeth-cleaning ingredient of our regular natural brand, then added a good amount of peppermint oil. The result was a nice clean, fresh taste, but the baking soda tang lingered. Marketing and sales shook their heads.

Kate and I stood our ground; it was a great natural ingredient.

But my managers were obstinate: "The numbers aren't there." They quoted retail market indicators like Nielsen, which showed no potential market for a baking soda toothpaste. I pointed out that the sales of "smokers' toothpastes" made by our competitors were suddenly on the rise, indicating that nonsmokers, too, were using them. Wouldn't the natural cleaning power of baking soda appeal to that market? We all know people who boast about their aged parents still having every tooth in their head when the only thing they brushed with their whole lives was baking soda, right out of the box. By creating a baking soda toothpaste, Kate and I argued, we were confirming a traditional belief in a *natural* product.

When Kate and I fought that same "flavor problem" battle in 1982 about whether our toothpaste needed a sweetener to succeed in supermarkets, we had come up with what we called a Five Day Flavor Test. On the panel of the trial-size box, we invited the consumer to try Tom's of Maine natural, unsweetened toothpaste for five days, then return to their old brand. We bet them that they would prefer the "clean, fresh taste" of our brand to our artificially sweetened competitors. Two-thirds of the people who took us up on that wager stayed with Tom's of Maine. Kate and I were convinced that people would buy a baking soda brand of toothpaste for the same reason.

In my imagination the product had always made sense. It cleaned teeth, it added a natural ingredient that was innovative for us, and it connected to tradition. It seemed perfect for Tom's of Maine. But my marketing and sales leaders still had their doubts. They were unable to imagine the possibilities because they had been trained to deal in the tangibles, to control and maximize them, and to identify the trends; using baking soda went against all their training.

Kate and I persisted, got some encouragement from some sampling, and eventually launched our new baking soda toothpaste. It was an instant success, without even drawing sales away from our other flavors—a total gain. By the end of the first year, it was making the same contribution to the company's sales as our number-one-selling item, spearmint toothpaste. That same year, Arm & Hammer launched its baking soda toothpaste with an eight-million-dollar advertising campaign and gained nearly eight percent of the total toothpaste business. Colgate followed with its own baking soda brand, with Lever Brothers and Procter & Gamble following. Today—three years after Tom's of Maine became a leader in the development of the product—20 percent of the market is baking soda toothpaste.

Kate and I had followed our instincts, in spite of the protestations of our own management "professionals," and we had been right. By the end of my first year at Harvard, I had learned to affirm those kinds of intuitions and the very values that had gotten us into the business in the first place—serving people with healthy ingredients from nature, taking care of our environment, and trying to treat people with respect: "I-Thou" and "being as relation." From the beginning, Tom's of Maine had put its values—*our* values—on the shelf, and growth and profits had followed.

RESOLVING

THE VALUES CLASH

The company, however, was no longer the "mom and pop" operation of its early days. Those same professionals with whom I was now disagreeing had helped us achieve our goals and, I felt, could help us go even further. But how could I continue to tap into their skills yet convince them as my executives to trust the kinds of intuitions and values that accounted for our original success? How could I wean them from their utilitarian tendencies? How could I get the Tom's of Maine board to understand the wisdom—and excitement—of our entrepreneurial ways? I wanted them all to know that Tom's of Maine could embody an alternative to the soulless, grim, numbers-dominated approach of American business as usual.

Since it was Martin Buber who had opened my eyes, I decided to let Buber open theirs. I invited Richard Niebuhr to visit Kennebunk to talk to our executives and officers. While I don't know if the board saw the irony in this, I certainly did: Nine months after I had escaped from Tom's of Maine to divinity school, I was bringing divinity school to Tom's of Maine.

THE BOARD OF DIRECTORS
MEETS MARTIN BUBER

I bought two dozen copies of *I and Thou* and brazenly sent them to every member of the board, to all my managers, and to several ministers in Kennebunk as well. I included a note explaining my enthusiasm for the book and an invitation to read it and then join Professor Richard Niebuhr of the Harvard Divinity School and me for a Sunday afternoon discussion. I was so fired up about my little seminar that I actually called around to the secretaries and told them to make sure Buber got into their bosses' briefcases.

Bringing Niebuhr up to Maine was a daring move on my part. I wasn't absolutely convinced that my business colleagues would share my enthusiasm for religious and philosophical ideas. I had no illusions that I could transform the business philosophies of my board members—among whom was the dean of a business school, other business professionals, and a Washington lawyer—by getting them to read a book and talk about it. But I was willing to risk their thinking me odd because I did want to arouse their curiosity about alternative ways of doing business. I hoped to inspire them to notice that the Tom's of Maine way of doing things may not be so primitive or "unprofessional" after all. Sure, we put a personal message on our product boxes; no, we didn't have a time clock for employees to punch; yeah, we did answer *all* our consumer mail. But for all these strange practices we were still a very successful company. I was hoping that Buber would prove to my tough-minded board that originality and intuition are not such bad assets to have.

Against the odds, my Buber strategy was a success. Professor Niebuhr charmed my board and the other hard-liners, and his lecture stimulated a general discussion about relationships in the world of business and about treating customers as more than statistics, as more than objects in one marketing category or another. Then we broke up into groups of four and five, including some local ministers and men and women from our management team, to discuss how we might

23

apply Buber's ideas to our lives and business practices. Many of these executives and board members were not accustomed to discussing philosophy and theology, but they found themselves exhilarated by the process. They finished the day satisfied and enthusiastic about their personal and professional revelations. Bill Schweitzer, the Washington lawyer and an old college friend (and one of the no-nonsense members of the board), said to me, "We've got to have more meetings like this. This was the most exciting thing I've done in a long time."

I agreed—it had been a great day. I had actually gotten a group of businesspeople to forget their charts and objectives for a time and reflect on what genuine relationships with each other, with employees, and with customers might look like. But what I didn't tell Bill was that my days at Harvard Divinity School were filled with this kind of intellectual exhilaration. Now that I had this additional reinforcement that my studies could actually fuel my business self, I was simply bubbling over with enthusiasm. Unlike most other students, I had a focus for my studies, an ever-present reference point for everything I heard, read, and thought about: Tom's of Maine.

PUTTING VALUES BACK
INTO THE DRIVER'S SEAT

I began to think about how I could transform Tom's of Maine into a company that could live its values—*my* values—and continue to grow. Kate and I, along with Dick Spencer, had begun the company in the belief that environmental protection and profit could be merged. We had all moved back to the land to find a better life for ourselves and our families. We practiced organic gardening and better nutrition with whole-grain foods, more vegetables, and less meat, as did our friends. Kate, Dick, and I had a *mission,* though we hadn't recognized it as such at the time because it was our life, the way we lived. In that first decade our commitment to using natural ingredients and serving our customers and employees—our *values*—had informed every decision we made at Tom's of Maine.

But between 1981 and 1986, as the company expanded into new markets, our values were pushed to the margin; growth and profit dominated business planning. "Professionalization" and "maximization" became the values that drove the company. I wanted to resuscitate our original values, bring respect for people and nature back into our management meetings and strategy sessions. But to do this effectively it was crucial for me to persuade my board and top executives that we all shared the same mission.

Tom, the man, had done a lot of thinking at Harvard. Now it was time for Tom's of Maine to do some serious thinking about the kind of company it really wanted to be. Did Tom's want to be merely another big packaged-goods company obsessed with increasing the numbers in its quarterly reports to stockholders? Or did it want to nurture the relationship it had with its customers and become a company that not only mouthed its values but *lived* them?

We had begun to explore some of those questions that summer Sunday after Niebuhr's lecture, but I needed to map out the next steps in my regeneration of Tom's. Seven months later, I suggested to the board that we focus on some long-range planning. We started talking, but by the spring I was convinced that to accomplish the change of mind I wanted in my colleagues, we needed a closely directed follow-up to the Buber seminar, this time to concentrate on the future of Tom's of Maine. I informed the board that I was considering organizing a two-day retreat for us all that would be a strategic planning meeting. We would focus on nothing less than what we believed our company to be and where we thought it ought to be going. They agreed.

I knew this could be no traditional skull session. Over the next few months, working with Kate and Pearl Rutledge, a board member who is a psychologist specializing in organizational development, we structured and discussed the shape of the meeting. As a result of Pearl's pointed and repeated question "What kind of outcomes do we want?" I soon realized that my ambitions for the retreat were large: I wanted to turn the conventional business planning process inside out and upside down.

Typically, companies meet in strategy sessions to formulate a business plan, then tack on some values to legitimate it. We had done it ourselves in 1981 when we created a "five-year plan" to grow beyond the shelves of health food stores. The Tom's of Maine board at that time wanted to maintain the company's original commitment to natural ingredients and its customers; but our main goal had been to increase our sales and profits.

I was now eager to reverse these priorities. In the group sessions, we would discuss how to shape the identity of the business according to what we valued. Instead of asking, "Where do we want to be in five years, and how do we get there?" I would ask, "Who are we?" and "What do we believe?" and "What is our mission?"

Since our experience the year before with applying philosophy and business values had been a good one, I figured another dose couldn't hurt. To get the board thinking about the nature of business in general, a couple of weeks before the meeting I sent each of them some sections from Immanuel Kant's writings about human freedom, self-interest, and enlightenment. I chose Kant, the great nineteenth-century German philosopher, because he had tried to give ethics a nonreligious foundation. A century after Enlightenment philosophers had made science and reason into their new God and at a time when the Industrial Revolution was in full swing, Kant had tried to reestablish goodness and worthiness as things worthwhile in themselves. Human beings should not be treated as *means* to some end, Kant famously taught, but as *ends in themselves*. In other words, we have to respect other people for who they are, not for what they can do for us. I was hoping that this view of how a moral person ought to act *in the world* would, like Buber's "I-Thou" concept, open up my board to the importance of values in business. I thought Kant's concept of freedom would help them think more easily about ways to break out of the confines of traditional capitalism's exclusive worship of the bottom line.

To assure them that I was not trying to lock them into some kind of ivory tower where they would lose all their business sense for some high-minded philosophical view of the world, I also sent around some excerpts from a new book called *Leadership and the Quest for Integrity* by Joseph L. Badaracco, Jr., who teaches at the Harvard

Business School, and Claremont's Richard R. Ellsworth. According to these professors of business, "What separates a leader from a competent professional manager is the ability to build an organization that is a source of self-fulfillment and personal integrity for its members." I was eager for my board members to know that even at the Harvard *Business* School, people were discussing the importance of shared values to the success of any company. Employees have to be motivated, values motivate people, and "ultimately values have a profound effect on the execution of a company strategy," write Badaracco and Ellsworth.

I also divulged my own feelings about the role of values in formulating a business strategy. I suggested tentatively that we might need to get our company values down on paper in the form of a mission statement. I even went so far as to offer my own vision of a company with such a mission:

> The mission of the company shapes the hopes, expectations, and aspirations of this business community in noneconomic terms. . . . The mission statement should provide some description of distinction in our purpose. Our point of view that natural ingredients are better for you than synthetic distinguishes us in one way. All in all, the mission should evoke our passion for risking resources in a competitive marketplace. . . .

It seemed a lofty goal, but I made it clear to the board that I wanted to take them off the hook. Tom's of Maine needed a mission statement not only to define its future but to help people move beyond trying to second-guess what Kate and I wanted. Finally, I wanted to allay the fear that by focusing on company values we might forget about company profits.

BUSINESSPEOPLE

DEFINING THE BUSINESS MISSION

The retreat was held in a resort hotel where the Kennebunk River meets the Atlantic Ocean, in June 1989. From the hotel, you could see the river running into the open ocean; sailboats and commercial crafts were moored below. The sun glistened on the saltwater tides of the river. It was almost too beautiful a place to hold a business meeting. But this awe-inspiring locale was part of the plan. In the context of such natural wonders people were bound to feel freer and would be less inclined to focus exclusively on the bottom line.

Professor Niebuhr, not unamused by his role as Tom's of Maine's official philosopher, made a return engagement, this time lecturing on Kant's concept of freedom. In his essay "On Enlightenment" Kant discussed the kind of "bondage" or "tutelage" (in other words, instruction) we subject ourselves to. Of course, Kant was referring to freedom from *political* bondage, but I was hoping that my board members would see an analogy to how businessmen are chained to the conventional tutelage of the business schools and packaged-goods firms, not to mention three hundred years of traditional capitalism. The purpose of business, the traditional doctrine goes, is profit, and profit alone. That, too, is a kind of tutelage, a bondage I definitely wanted our company to break out of.

Niebuhr's lecture on Kant's ideas helped move everyone's thinking away from the nuts-and-bolts strategies of typical business planning sessions to the tougher, more philosophical questions about defining our business values. Before we could act as a company, we would first have to know what we believed in as a company. A general discussion period ensued.

"Whose beliefs are we talking about?" asked a board member. "Yours," I answered. "Your beliefs as you take part in this meeting and work in this business." *In this business*—that was essential. I hoped to make clear that this was not an exercise in separating who we were from what Tom's of Maine was. On the contrary, we were all agents of both—of ourselves and of the company. To be clear about the company's beliefs, we would have to be clear about our own. And to have a sense of who we were, we would have to know what we believed.

Our mandate was to answer two questions: "Who are we?" and "What is our mission?" We broke up into small groups of four or so. The talk ranged widely over different areas. We discussed how we treated the people who worked for Tom's of Maine, whether there should be a profit-sharing plan, and whether everyone should own stock; we talked about the importance of rewarding both individual performance and teamwork, how the company could do more for the community, and how we wanted to create natural products that helped sustain the natural world. We filled large sheets of newsprint with our beliefs about business and what its mission should be that we later hung on the walls for all to look at together.

As we reviewed our beliefs, everyone was stunned at how little had been said in any of the groups about the place of profit in our mission. It *was* there, but we all obviously had other expectations about business that we needed to focus on. We *all* had higher aims and aspirations. But that was the point of the meeting. I had brought Niebuhr back to talk about freedom so that the board and management could literally free themselves from their business *habits*—their obsession with discipline, control, focus, maximization, and profit—that had supplanted their business *goals*. I wanted them to consider the possibility that besides making money they were also accountable to their own beliefs and values.

But what about those business buzzwords *net profit, market share, operating efficiency*? A few *had* kept in mind these more familiar goals of business while deferring to me and the primary goal of our meeting. Bill Schweitzer (who as my fraternity brother was less intimidated by the founder/CEO than some of the others) finally dared to raise what other people in the room had doubtless been thinking: "You've got to talk more about profit. You can't do anything without it, and you've got to name it prominently among your beliefs." Others then admitted to some discomfort with the tone of our discussion, with our preoccupation with, as one put it, "soft and feely issues" such as human dignity and the common good and the environment. As one of my top executives also warned, "There's no business without profit."

I agreed. But I pointed out that profit was only a means to the end of fulfilling the company's beliefs, its higher aims that we had just named: to do good for our customers, to treat our employees well, to contribute to our community, to protect the environment, and in general to tread lightly on the human spirit. The ethics of Tom's of Maine, according to Tom, was that the financial success of the owners comes last. I wanted them to know where I stood: Profit was my goal, too, but not my only goal. I wanted to change the way we saw our work and the way we did our work. The business was to be a vehicle for uniting values and work.

Another board member piped up, "Don't we mean to say that we believe in all of these things—social responsibility as well as profit?" That provoked more discussion and writing and editing, and some disagreement. But the creative energy in the room was intense. We recognized that all these relationships—to the customer, the employee, the environment, the community, *and* the bottom line—could be integrated. We had reclaimed the values of the company, but we had also decided that the bottom-line habits of traditional business were no longer going to drive our company. The men and women in that room cared about their responsibility to the environment and the community as well as about profit. Two board members tried to come up with a synthesis of the different lists of beliefs from each circle. And suddenly, two days of talk came together into one concise sentence:

 We believe that the company can be financially successful, environmentally sensitive, and socially responsible.

It was a powerful moment. It was as if everyone on the board, the diehard "profiteers" as well as the "soft-and-feelies," had merged into one mind to recognize that Tom's of Maine could be committed to both visions, profit *and* social responsibility. We had knocked King Profit off the throne. While we were not about to turn Tom's of Maine into a nonprofit company—far from it—we *were* stating that we would try to go about our business of making money without compromising our commitment to honoring the world and the life in it. We had made respect for nature and people into cornerstones of our new business strategy. We had confirmed our special identity as a company.

Afterward, one skeptical participant sidled up to me to say, "I wasn't sure where you were going for a while, but it was great." The retreat ended with a sense of real accomplishment. We had done our work. We felt pushed and expanded. We had grown. We had disagreed, but we were unified. We had even had fun. And most important, we now had lists of beliefs we could take away from the retreat and shape into a final statement of the mission of Tom's of Maine.

To include the entire company in this process, a few months later, the employees of Tom's of Maine gathered under a large tent on the company grounds with a draft of the statement of beliefs and the mission in their hands. They were invited to review it sentence by sentence and to offer comments or suggestions. (We provided pencils and index cards.) I then appointed a committee of employees representing all departments of the company to put this material into the form of recommendations and to meet with an editorial group from the board to negotiate the differences. Three months after the board had sat down to discuss how Kant's concept of freedom related to the future of Tom's of Maine, it approved final drafts of the two statements:

TOM'S OF MAINE
STATEMENT OF BELIEFS

WE BELIEVE that both human beings and nature have inherent worth and deserve our respect.

WE BELIEVE in products that are safe, effective, and made of natural ingredients.

WE BELIEVE that our company and our products are unique and worthwhile, and that we can sustain these genuine qualities with an ongoing commitment to innovation and creativity.

WE BELIEVE that we have a responsibility to cultivate the best relationships possible with our co-workers, customers, owners, agents, suppliers, and our community.

WE BELIEVE in providing employees with a safe and fulfilling work environment, and an opportunity to grow and learn.

WE BELIEVE that our company can be financially successful while behaving in a socially responsible and environmentally sensitive manner.

TOM'S OF MAINE

MISSION STATEMENT

TO SERVE our customers by providing safe, effective, innovative, natural products of high quality.

TO BUILD a relationship with our customers that extends beyond product usage to include full and honest dialogue, responsiveness to feedback, and the exchange of information about products and issues.

TO RESPECT, value, and serve not only our customers, but also our co-workers, owners, agents, suppliers, and our community; to be concerned about and contribute to their well-being, and to operate with integrity so as to be deserving of their trust.

TO PROVIDE meaningful work, fair compensation, and a safe, healthy work environment that encourages openness, creativity, self-discipline, and growth.

TO ACKNOWLEDGE the value of each person's contribution to our goals, and to foster teamwork in our tasks.

TO BE DISTINCTIVE in products and policies which honor and sustain our natural world.

TO ADDRESS community concerns, in Maine and around the globe, by devoting a portion of our time, talents, and resources to the environment, human needs, the arts, and education.

TO WORK TOGETHER to contribute to the long-term value and sustainability of our company.

TO BE A PROFITABLE AND SUCCESSFUL COMPANY, while acting in a socially and environmentally responsible manner.

The Free and Responsible Corporation
(A Social Perspective to Private Incentive)

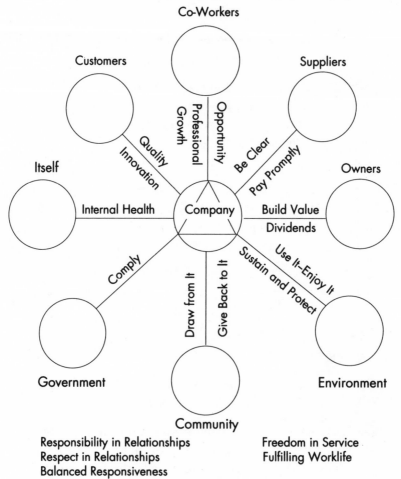

Responsibility in Relationships
Respect in Relationships
Balanced Responsiveness

Freedom in Service
Fulfilling Worklife

To illustrate that the identity of Tom's of Maine was based on the power of relationship, I had the rough drawing of my own response to Jonathan Edwards's view that "being is relation" shaped into a graphic.

Over the course of a year we had articulated our beliefs and defined our Mission. We had affirmed that we wanted to work with these values day in and day out. We wanted them to live for us every day of the week, not go dormant on Monday mornings. We had refined and practiced them in our heads and on paper. Now all we had to do was live them.

INCORPORATING YOUR VALUES INTO YOUR CORPORATE BUSINESS STRATEGY

How to begin? Like much that has been successful at Tom's of Maine, we explored our identity and defined a mission that squared with it. Winging it is, it seems, our specialty. But in the process, we learned a lot. For any business leader who is eager to try to merge a company's values with strategy, here are some key steps to take:

1. Identify your personal and professional values. How? The simplest way to articulate your values is in "I believe" statements. For example:

   - "I believe that profit is essential to a healthy business."

   - "I believe that people are worthy of respect."

   - "I believe our business should benefit this community."

2. Raise the questions that will provoke answers about beliefs and values, force them to the surface. Don't be afraid to be too general, or "philosophical." (You are questioning the nature of your business, its essence, and that, after all, is what philosophy is all about.)

3. Be willing to ask the big questions. For example:

- "Is business only quantitative—about the numbers?"

- "Is it qualitative—about values?"

- "Is it about both?"

- "Do we want our business plans to include what we value?"

- "Should there be some coherence between what we value in business and what we value in our lives outside the office?"

4. Remember that this kind of "values audit" needs to be inclusive. The values articulated by someone earning $100,000 and sitting in a boardroom may be very different from the values of someone making $15,000. Both need to be heard and taken into account.

5. To help people break out of the confines of typical business discussions, bring in someone from outside the company who can speak about values. Inviting an eminent theologian like Richard Niebuhr to address the board of directors of Tom's of Maine had a tremendous impact on everyone. His presence was so unusual for a business meeting that it gave a refreshing depth and seriousness to our discussions. Also include some reading material that raises ethical issues. For example:

- *Leadership and the Quest for Integrity,* by Joseph L. Badaracco, Jr., and Richard R. Ellsworth

- *Corporate Ethics and Strategic Planning,* by R. Edward Freeman and Daniel R. Gilbert, Jr.

- "On Enlightenment," in Immanuel Kant's *On History*

- *I and Thou,* by Martin Buber

- *Essay on the Mind,* by Jonathan Edwards

- First Corinthians, by Saint Paul

6. The same kind of "intellectual-in-residence" may not work for every business. Find someone who can speak to the values everyone holds in common, who can address the whole person, not just the analytical business issues on the table. Tom's tried a religious thinker who could talk about a philosophical issue—liberty or identity—that might be relevant to business. Your company might need a social worker, a doctor, or someone else who can speak with passion about a powerful life question.

7. Work in groups of four to six to answer the questions, one at a time: "Who are we?" and "What are we about?" Make sure each group is evenly balanced so that one isn't packed with all talkers while another comprises only listeners.

8. Once you think you have answers to these questions, write them down. Edit them. Invite companywide comments. Edit them again. Send the final draft to the board.

9. Implement these beliefs—your *mission*—into your business strategy. You've thought about it—now give it a try.

10. Remember, nothing is written in stone. Your first attempt might not work. You're making a huge change in the way you do business; it will take some getting used to for everyone. Being a pioneer is never easy. Living the mission at Tom's of Maine didn't happen in a day—hardly (as I will show in the next chapter).

LIVING THE

MISSION

F orging our Mission had taken a year of thought and talk, and some disagreement, but now we had the makings of a new kind of American company. The board of Tom's of Maine and its executives had agreed to try doing business in a revolutionary way. I was eager to prove to the world that the company's new Mission to manage for profit and the common good could work. So with the Mission and Beliefs statements in place, my message to the company was, "Let's go!"

But the rest of the company was not quite so eager to change according to the guidelines of what they called "Tom's Mission." One day a truckload of toothpaste arrived at the warehouse from the production plant. On one of the pallets, scribbled in large letters, was the message: "Mission Impossible."

Looking back on those days, I would say the company joker had a point. Living the Mission did not prove to be as easy as I had thought. At Tom's we eventually learned that very little happens during the first year of implementing a mission. That's not because people are opposed to the values that have been articulated. It's because they are waiting to see if the company leadership is really serious about this change, if they mean it, if it is really going to grab hold. Employees know that companies are political entities. Like any savvy executive, they want to know which way the wind is blowing before they commit themselves. So before I get to the stories of how we profited from our Mission, let me tell you about some of the problems we faced and how we developed new ways of managing and adapting to these changes we'd brought on ourselves.

Our initial steps in making the Mission happen were halting, even stumbling. We formed a Mission Implementation Committee that was representative of the whole company—a woman from the production line, a man from the warehouse, someone from the secretaries, someone from marketing, and so on. The task of the committee, headed by Frances Hancock, a fellow student from the divinity school who had joined the company as coordinator of community life, was to figure out how every department would realize the Mission. It was only the first step, yet it turned out to be the most difficult.

For almost a decade, the company had been operating pretty much as a traditional American business. I had underestimated the magnitude of the effort it would take to get our clever young MBAs and experienced packaged-goods executives, with their taste for rational analysis and their eye for the bottom line, to get back in tune with the values that had motivated Kate and me to get into the personal-care-products business in the first place. I just hadn't realized how ingrained the utilitarian spirit had become.

Tom's was then a top-down company. All the departments were headed by experienced professional managers—every one of them a man. It was a male culture in which aggressive competition and making the numbers took precedence over caring about what the employees thought. The Mission's success depended on communication between departments, but there was no structure in place to encourage such communication. Like most companies, Tom's was divided into different turfs (marketing, sales, production, finance, and the like), and their chieftains were defensive to say the least.

But the biggest problem was me—my head was too far out in front of management's. While the board and I were committed to this driving new philosophy, management had a long way to go before they even got the feel of this change in direction, never mind understanding how to implement it. The employees, too, were confused and intimidated by the prospect of change. The company was suddenly reflecting two very different value systems—the traditional utilitarian style of my managers and the people-directed principles of the Mission. Could utility and respect for others live in the same company? Could profit and professionalism, competition and compassion, coexist?

Frances asked me to remove myself from the Mission implementation process, explaining that some of the hourly employees were shaking in their boots just to be in the same room with the big boss himself. In fact, fear and distrust were rampant throughout the company, among management as well as labor. I couldn't believe it! If some outside consultant whom I was paying $1,500 a day had told me that my employees were intimidated by a nice guy like me, I would have thrown them out. But Frances was no consultant; she was a friend who had taken the same courses as I had, discussed the same issues. She didn't view me as "president of Tom's of Maine," and so she had no problem coming into my office and leveling with me.

Because Frances was new to the business world and inexperienced in the games of corporate hierarchy, she was also able to cut through some smokescreens and get to the core of the problems of implementation. While I had been listening to the heads of the departments, Frances had been listening to the employees who have to do the bidding of their department heads. Her religious training and life experience had sensitized her to the needs—and fears—of the powerless. According to Frances, the employees felt that this new "Mission thing" was asking them to shoulder a large load. They wanted to do a great job, but they didn't have the power, didn't have the respect, weren't getting the direction they needed—except to make the numbers. In short, the employees didn't believe this new Mission was for real.

I was stunned. Eager to bring my company into a new way of doing business, I didn't want to hear that not everyone was as gung-ho as I was. But as Frances and I discussed how to get around the resistance to change and the confusion over what the Mission really meant, I realized she was right. I had to convince my employees that *they* were likely to benefit the most from the changes implied in the Mission. I also had to get my executives to change their way of viewing business—or else trade them in. "You've got a lot of listening to do," Frances said to me. We both knew the passage in the Gospel according to Mark where Jesus, frustrated with the inability of his disciples to understand his mission, says angrily: "Do you not yet perceive or understand? Or are your hearts hardened? Having eyes do you not see, and having ears do you not hear?" In one conversation with Frances, I said, "Right now we need a new metaphor for management in our changing company—we need to be an ear." We needed to take in and listen to all the messages from all levels of employees. We needed to see and hear them.

LISTENING THE
MISSION INTO REALITY

"Just let the Mission seep down," advised one member of the board. "Give it a chance to soak into the company." He suggested having "more company gatherings" where people could get to know each other better. The staff was now scattered among three different buildings, and a lot of people didn't even recognize their fellow employees. To bring people closer together in plain, simple fellowship, we interrupted a normal workday and asked all the employees, fifty strong, to meet at a local resort hotel, where we could all have a swim in an indoor pool, eat some pizza, and talk. The plan was to help them relax as a company group and then hold a listening session in smaller groups. Basically, we wanted people to get to know each other as people and not as job categories. To break the ice in the groups, Pearl suggested each person tell three stories about their lives, one of which would be a lie. The group would try to guess which story was a lie.

Talk about revelations! Paul, a quiet middle-aged man who processes our sales orders, said for his first story that he used to be a policeman. Story two was that he had become convinced that someone he arrested had been unjustly set free, and he had written a novel about the case. The final story from Paul, who has a shock of prematurely white hair, was about the joys of being a grandfather. Not one person in the group guessed that Paul had lied about being a grandfather. It was amazing: The person at our order-processing desk was an ex-cop and a novelist, and we had had no idea!

In addition to the lying game, each group discussed two issues from the Mission Statement:

> To respect, value and serve not only our customers, but also our co-workers . . . to be concerned about and contribute to their well-being, and to operate with integrity so as to be deserving of their trust. To acknowledge the value of each person's contributions to our goals, and to foster teamwork in our tasks.

Getting together to listen, we heard plenty. Some people were happy with the company, others were disappointed, and many had some major gripes, a few of them on the mark. But it was a terrific day. We wrote the comments on large sheets of newsprint and posted them around the company, the praises as well as the damns:

- I'm grateful to work for a company that cares enough to listen to my needs.

- I don't feel I'm respected here.

- Tar the road—the potholes are ruining my new car.

- I'm a human being, not a human doing!

- We need a company newsletter.

- We're human, all too human.

- The building is a mess.
- We need a childcare facility.
- We need a recycling center here.
- Let's have more fun events with our families.
- How about a suggestion box for all locations?

The get-together gave us a lot of concrete things to work on, some goals to shoot for. We went to work. I had banners made of our Statement of Beliefs and hung them at different locations, reminders amid all the problems and pressures of life and work of the beliefs we wanted to put into action. We made arrangements to pay part of any employee's fees at local childcare centers, and we authorized a newsletter. The road was tarred, the building was repainted inside and out, changes in safety procedures were made, and a suggestion box was put in place.

The Mission had been institutionalized. High-minded words such as "respecting our co-workers" had been embodied in a smooth new road and financial aid for child care. The employees saw that the Mission wasn't just blowing smoke.

I had learned an important lesson: No matter how good it is to get your beliefs and Mission down on paper, they're likely to stay on paper unless you make a major effort to sell them to your constituents. Our *intentional* effort to get to know each other, to open up the Tom's community, made a huge difference in showing us all—me as well as my employees—how to live our Mission as a company. The results were so obvious that we soon hired a vice-president of community life to make sure, among other things, that the dialogue between management and workers continued.

As a company practice, we started to take time out at work for occasional celebrations and observances—of births and deaths and retirements—that would bring us together into a genuine community where employees knew their co-workers. We would stop the manufacturing machines and gather everyone informally for a disarming, uncomplicated hour of food and drink and conversation. People from different departments saw one another for the first time in months. We began to understand and deal with life and work issues as a family, and that itself was evidence of the work of the Mission among us.

THE MISSION TAKES HOLD

Soon we realized, as one employee put it, that "the beliefs and Mission were what Tom's of Maine had always really been about, only now they were on purpose." To be sure, some employees resisted such intentional efforts "to be good" by not showing up for company events or skipping office celebrations; they felt that they already were good, and that good people would do good things without prompting. But we persisted in making it part of our company identity to treat ourselves and others as people—as spouses, parents, and family members who experience confusion, problems, joys, celebrations, and sorrows—and to encourage people to put their own real souls and selves into their work.

Tom's of Maine has since grown to eighty-five people, and we still have these company get-togethers. Even in a company of 180 or 1,800, I believe it's possible to establish smaller units connected to one another by common values. We all need to feel part of something, some entity that is, intellectually and emotionally, both manageable and imaginable. Perhaps the Native American idea of clans—groups of affiliates through which people understand themselves—are what large corporations need to foster to create the kind of sense of belonging—the bonds—that we need.

Eventually the banners came down, but by that time the Mission and Beliefs statements had become part of our regular training process every six months, for new employees as well as old ones. Once filled with distrust of management and skeptical of the Mission, employees now began implementing the Mission in their own ways. For example:

As members of the marketing department faced growing amounts of consumer mail, they asked themselves, "If we believe in the company's Mission 'to build a relationship with our customers,' how should we respond to this?" After some careful thought about what the Mission meant, they recommended a plan for expanding the department, which eventually grew from a staff of two to fifteen.

A group of manufacturing employees initiated, on their own, recycling of corrugated boxes. They convinced suppliers to ship in reusable cartons that could go back and forth between Tom's and our suppliers. They also set out to find every possible way for us to reduce our own waste and minimize overpackaging.

One employee took on the job of working with a local soils engineer to solve an embarrassing and destructive wastewater problem we had. Our leaching system was forever failing, causing process waste to ooze into the neighboring woods. They devised a natural filter system that used peat moss. The change was dramatic, imaginative, and environmentally responsible. It was also in concert with our Mission.

It was as if the Mission had given these employees permission to release the creativity and social responsibility that had been bottled up inside them. The Mission soon became their guide, part of the way they thought. The Mission even invaded my own subconscious. One night I had a dream.

I dreamed about putting large displays of fruit in the warehouse and production areas for employees to snack on. In my dream I was trying to stack the fruit in dazzling arrays—that kept falling apart. The next day I told my managers about the dream, and within a week baskets of fruit were made available so that employees could grab an apple or orange or banana at any time during the workday. I saw the fruit as a simple affirmation of the dignity of human life, above and beyond just our capacity to produce. The employees saw it as proof that the company cared about them. They pitched in, shopping for the fruit and arranging it in baskets in various locations around the company. In fact, no expensive bonuses or even the new 401(k) retirement/profit-sharing plan has made such a difference in company morale or fostered as much trust and respect as providing the free baskets of fruit. Eighteen months later, employees initiated a ten-week seminar on nutrition, which caused the consumption of fruit to jump again.

A LESSON LEARNED

A mission statement can give people a chance to take their own initiatives, even inspire them to try something new. But this kind of action-oriented attitude will not happen overnight. Once our company had agreed on what its Mission was, I had assumed it would be put into action. I was convinced that my managers and employees would be inspired and respond enthusiastically. Immediately. Instead, they were frightened and distrustful until they saw it was for real.

Accepting the Mission turned out to be a lot easier for our new employees. They had had no experience of the company during its most "professionalized" years. From the first job interview, which is centered on the Mission, candidates for employment learn immediately what the company is about, what it believes in.

We found that the presence of the Mission even in that problem-fraught first year had a snowball effect. People love working in a company whose values they share; and people love working with other people who are so committed to acting on their beliefs.

We learned another thing as the Mission took hold: Expect the unexpected. When you put your beliefs in black and white and when you articulate a company's mission, your words can sneak up and catch you unawares. They can also cost you some money.

PUTTING OUR MONEY
WHERE OUR MOUTH IS

Four or so months after the Mission seemed to have taken hold at Tom's, I was giving a speech before the Harvard University Environment Club. I talked about the need to make values part of a business strategy, how we can still do well by doing good, how utility is not the only measure of business, and how respecting humans and the environment deserves a prime place in the goals of every businessperson. I talked about Buber, Edwards, Kant—gave my whole pitch. Then I invited questions from the audience.

A young business school student raised his hand. "Do you plan to eliminate the outer sleeve on your deodorant in order to reduce your use of paper?" he asked, with genuine curiosity and no evidence of hostility. I explained that Tom's had a responsibility to inform its customers, and the deodorant sleeve was where we conveyed that information. I took another question.

But that question about the deodorant sleeve became a guilty echo in my conscience. The student was right: We ought to have been reducing the amount of paper we used. It was already there in the Mission, embodied clearly in two points: "To be distinctive in products and policies which honor and sustain our natural world," and "To be a profitable and successful company, while acting in a socially and environmentally responsible manner." Back at the office, I discussed the sleeve problem. Katie Shisler, my then-new vice-president of marketing, pointed out that if we took the Mission seriously, we would have to recognize that the sleeve presented us with a moral dilemma—the informational value of the deodorant sleeve versus the fact that it wasted paper. She recommended discontinuing the sleeve.

I conceded that if we were to be different from the big packaged-goods companies that were notorious for bulking up their containers and packages as a ploy to increase their shelf presence, we would have to justify the size of the deodorant sleeve. My justification was information. Every Tom's of Maine product has to explain what its ingredients are and their purpose; we also tell the Tom's of Maine story on the sleeve, about how Kate and I moved to Maine for a better life, couldn't find natural products, and decided to create our own. The package also alerts customers to our Mission Statement. Over the years, our consumer research had shown that customers choose our products *for* this information. If the sleeve were to go, Katie would have to devise an alternative way to get all that information onto the deodorant package.

That's just what she did, with the help of an interdepartmental team that included an engineer, a purchasing agent, and the production manager. They came up with the idea of an accordion-fold leaflet filled with the standard Tom's information—it could be lifted from the container as a separate booklet to be used in the home. The base label remained on the deodorant package.

The new deodorant package was a winner. It seemed to embody the Mission. Not only was it creative, but it proved that the Mission was not just some billboard of company slogans to be stuck on the wall, like a high school basketball coach's list of pieties for a winning team. The new package proved that the Mission could actually *solve problems*.

Equally significant, the evolution of the deodorant "outsert" was the first time the company had ever solved a problem *interdepartmentally*, notwithstanding some bruised egos in the process. It was not lost on me and other managers that it had taken a relative newcomer—a woman—to break down the walls between departments. Among our once male-dominated managerial group, intracompany competition had seemed a necessary way of life, turf battles a part of the natural energy of any company. Katie had proved that members of different departments could come together into a special creative group and achieve an important goal for the whole company.

Solving the deodorant-sleeve problem was a long, intensive, and exhausting process. In many ways it was symbolic of Tom's of Maine's effort to live its Mission. Success didn't begin to show itself until eighteen months after the board approved the Beliefs and Mission Statements. I estimate that it took two to three years for this fundamental change in the values of the company to take hold. We had begun in the dark, not knowing how long we would need to change our ways of doing business or what the results would be.

One thing we certainly learned was that good people will take a good idea and make good on it—if you expect them to. That is the wisdom of the Mission. Once its values take hold of the company community, informing it and inspiring it, the Mission is bound to stretch its embrace to the community at large.

LIVING THE MISSION
IN THE OUTSIDE COMMUNITY

 To address community concerns, in Maine
and around the globe . . .
THE TOM'S OF MAINE MISSION STATEMENT

Once the Mission seemed embedded safely in the consciousness of the company, we were ready to get involved in the affairs of the community we lived in. (International involvement would have to wait until we had tended to our own backyard.) To send a message about the company's commitment to the community, I donated $25,000 to the town of Kennebunk for the purchase of curbside recycling bins. Our gift, in turn, encouraged additional grants from the town and the State of Maine, and thus made a recycling program in Kennebunk possible.

That first step into corporate philanthropy generated a new policy at Tom's: a kind of corporate "tithing"—a commitment to distribute a proportion of our annual pretax profits to support education, the arts and humanities, environmental research and protection, and human-need projects such as shelters and programs for the handicapped. Our tithing began at five percent, soon went to seven, and is now at ten percent.

Requests for donations quickly poured in, creating an additional burden on management. We resisted setting up a foundation, preferring to keep donations to worthy causes a company project. We even set up the grants program so that ten percent of the company's total giving would go to community needs chosen by the employees themselves. The overall responsibility for managing our grants program and learning more about the groups seeking our help was turned over to Colleen Myers, our new vice-president of community life. As of this writing, we have received many more worthy requests for donations than we have the money for. But the day will come when Tom's of Maine will be giving away one million dollars of profits before taxes. When I first raised the idea of donating that $25,000 to

Kennebunk for a recycling program, eyebrows went up among the company leadership. Three years of tithing later, donations have become a normal, though very exciting, company practice.

The ten percent tithing is giving for the sake of giving, not as a means for good public relations. The decisions about who gets how much are left up to the community life department. But in addition to the ten percent, we set aside part of the marketing department's budget for sponsoring projects that affirm the values of Tom's of Maine. The company has underwritten locally National Public Radio's *Morning Edition* and *All Things Considered* and co-underwritten a public television series about practical efforts among Americans to respond to the environmental crisis. We've also made contributions to support local events such as a marathon race and an AIDS awareness conference. Finally, the company's commitment to the environment has inspired us to fund projects by Native American groups in Maine and in the Province of New Brunswick, across the border.

PROFITING FROM THE MISSION

During that first two-day retreat in 1989, the main concern among some members of my board was that while managing for the common good might be socially responsible, would it be *profitable*? Three years after the Mission went into place, we had a firm answer to that question: Tom's could manage for profit *and* for the common good.

Despite a national economic recession, sales of Tom's of Maine products increased by 31 percent and profits increased by 40 percent in 1992. This was an even stronger performance than the previous five years' average annual rate of 25 percent growth in sales and profits. By the end of 1992, Tom's had entered successfully into new markets up and down the West Coast, from Seattle to San Diego, increased our share of old markets, and produced strong balance sheets across the board. In the meantime we had introduced companywide retirement savings and profit-sharing plans, childcare benefits, and parental leave—all within a company doubling in sales size every three years. Our clear sense of identity and purpose had helped us flourish financially. It has also guided us in making some very tough financial decisions, like the renovation of the deodorant sleeve.

We ended up having an even more expensive problem with the deodorant itself. Eager to improve our Honeysuckle Deodorant, we added lichen to the existing coriander, both of which are natural antimicrobials, thus doubling the deodorant's odor-eating power. Because of our corporate goal of decreasing our dependence on petroleum, we replaced a petroleum derivative in the deodorant (propylene glycol) with a vegetable-based glycerin. After a favorable response in tests among an in-house group, we put the new reformulation on the shelves.

Within two months the first complaints began, then increased exponentially over the next several weeks. Scores of angry customers were on the telephone to tell us that their deodorant was conking out halfway through the day. A quick series of consumer tests confirmed that half of our customers were pleased, and half definitely were not. We went back to the lab and increased the amount of the lichen and coriander for better deodorant protection.

But the complaints didn't stop, and the heat from customers and stores soon demoralized the marketing and sales departments. We finally decided to put effectiveness before our principle of decreasing on petroleum and replaced the glycerin with the propylene glycol. We sent samples to two hundred of our angriest customers, and they loved it. Marketing and sales recommended a complete recall of the weak deodorant. To justify their decision, they pointed to the Mission, which stated the company's aim "to serve our customers by providing safe, effective, innovative natural products of high quality." By that measure, the deodorant—with the addition of the petroleum ingredient, the most effective product we had ever made—did not make the grade.

A product recall would cost $400,000—a significant bite, to say the least, in our anticipated profits for the year. We had a genuine moral dilemma—profits versus values. I pointed out that the Mission was not a one-sided document; it also calls on the company to respect the stockholders and all other financially interested parties. (I was not unaware of the irony—here was the values-oriented CEO reminding his marketing and sales department of the bottom line!) If we were to admit failure, we'd have to rein in plans in the works to crank up our successful ventures. My managers agreed to slow down growth and reduce marketing investments that were already in the works in order to assure a respectable profit for the year. It was a more cautious approach that placed profit goals before growth-rate goals, but it still protected the trust of our customers and the aspirations of our shareholders.

I authorized the $400,000 recall and thus said good-bye to 30 percent of our projected annual profits. It was a painful decision to make, but our sense of identity as a corporation committed to safety, effectiveness, and trust as well as profits showed us the way out of the crisis. Our ideals won out. The Mission held up to the test of its central belief: "The company can be financially successful, while behaving in a socially responsible and environmentally sensitive manner."

There was one catch: What to do with the old inventory? Depositing it in the dump would create a serious environmental problem. Colleen Myers came up with a happy solution: A national organization that worked with the homeless said it wanted the product—in spite of its marginal effectiveness—as part of its program to retrain people in personal hygiene habits.

But Tom's had disappointed thousands of loyal customers. We wrote to the two thousand who had complained, explaining what had happened and apologizing. We gave them a free sample of the new formulation, and 98 percent liked it and expressed their appreciation both for the new deodorant and for how the company had handled itself. Someone was listening.

The Mission had left us no choice. Leaving a weak product on the shelves would have risked the faith and trust of customers and employees alike. How could we expect our employees to live by the Mission if the company itself threw it aside? Our values and beliefs as a company helped put the crisis into perspective.

It also sharpened our awareness of our markets and the need to be creative in reaching them.

ALWAYS IN PROCESS—

THE MISSION AND THE COMPANY

Like many small companies, Tom's was awed by the MBA degree. We had assumed in our middle years that graduates of the best business schools in the land (Harvard, Dartmouth's Tuck School, Stanford) knew everything there was to know about business, just as many people look to a newly minted M.D. to know everything about healing the body. In our own naiveté, we simply deferred too much to the mystique of the MBA. What we didn't realize was that although these young MBAs had been well-schooled in theory, their knowledge of business was only from the point of view of the classroom, and the "case study" was their guide. In an entrepreneurial hothouse like Tom's, where the business changes significantly every few years, day-to-day business is a trial-and-error process. An entrepreneurial company like Tom's is nothing like the human body, with its vital organs always working in the same location; the MBA working at Tom's for six years is likely to walk into the office one morning and find a whole new company—its departments and functions redefined and reorganized. There are no paradigms except experience, intuition, and creativity.

Our new marketing goals included an advertising campaign that required us to move for the first time into television and print advertising. Trouble was, we couldn't afford it. But we were convinced that the new media campaign was so creative and promising that we had to find a way to bankroll it. The normal marketing response to this dilemma would be to use available dollars to implement the more costly creative campaign in fewer regions than we had previously broadcast our old radio ads. But we came up with something less "rational". We could finance the company's long-standing commitment to marketing on a regional basis by a *national* media strategy. By advertising on CNN and in select national magazines, we were able to develop new markets and gain dollars from new distribution that we could funnel back into a more intense newspaper strategy in our prime regional markets. Thus, ironically, Tom's regional strategy was financed by a national strategy.

It is the kind of ingenious remedy that you do not learn about in business school. This kind of business creativity is learned the hard way, in the trenches, where a company has to manage successfully with limited resources. I'm not saying that theory doesn't have its place. Tom's has benefited from new ideas coming out of the business schools as well as from theories from divinity school. But the kind of MBAs we want are those who can bring their theories and experience to the company and still be willing to learn from *our* experience.

MEASURING UP TO THE MISSION

Living and managing by values also showed us where the Mission Statement fell short. One of the most glaring defects was its lack of specific expectations of competence among our employees. How should we handle firing employees who weren't coming through in their jobs? Or what if an executive was committed in every fiber of his being to the Mission but just couldn't cut it? With business *doubling* every three years, within six years many people's abilities are severely tested.

Inevitably, some employees—at every level of the company, line workers as well as executives—are not going to be able to keep up with such major changes. Some will be unable to learn new skills; others may be unwilling. One of the toughest jobs I've had at Tom's has been to fire people who served the company well and for a long time. But in each case, from top executives and middle managers to valued supervisors and secretaries, expectations of them had changed because the company had become four times larger. Although they had once qualified for a particular job and been successful at it, they were no longer working effectively. The Mission Statement that we had designed did not take into account this kind of change. It provided no guidance.

Instead, the Mission's call to "respect human dignity" only clouded the issue. How did firing someone "respect" his dignity? While the statement suggested that we had financial obligations to any employee who was terminated, it did not make clear that, no matter what values the company was committed to, competence was a daily responsibility for everyone at Tom's, top to bottom; employees had to be willing to improve their skills and grow, and management had to provide the funds and training to make that possible— something we were not doing enough of. The employees most likely to prosper at Tom's are perpetual students, and the company has to contribute to their education with time, money, and direction.

The board agreed, and we proceeded to edit the Mission. Almost four years after the original drafts were presented to the company, the board proposed this addition to our Statement of Beliefs:

 We believe that competence is an essential means of sustaining our values in a competitive marketplace.

To the Mission Statement, we added the goal:

 To value, contribute to, and require a high level of competence in the work community.

We assembled the company once again and presented these new principles. I emphasized the importance of being very good at what we do in order to maintain a competitive advantage. Again, we broke up into small editing groups—and ran into an incredible amount of resistance. "We feel we're being judged," people said. "We feel our managers need to manage better." They demanded clear job descriptions, regular evaluations, and more training. "We feel like we're being called incompetent," they said. Clearly, we had touched a nerve.

Colleen assembled an editing committee whose job was to provide feedback to the board and its editing committee, just as we had done when we first drafted the Mission. The company leadership was willing to repeat the process and be the ear to all employees, no matter their job, income level, or standing in the company.

Some employees rejected the principle of competence, preferring to talk about "standards of excellence." That reminded me of what Jonathan Edwards had written about "excellency." For Edwards, this quality of excellency is a "consent of spirits" to one another, such as love or respect or gratitude. According to Edwards, "the more the consent is the more the excellency." In business, the proof of excellency is when a customer says, "Great idea, great product, thank you. I'm grateful." In the words of our employees, the standard of excellence is defined as "a high level of commitment, skill, and effectiveness."

As I thought about the employees' views and my own, I saw that their perspective recognized a standard of excellence in their work. I saw "a high level of competence" as being a necessary precursor to excellence, however, and a more explicit calling. Without competent work from its employees, a business cannot confidently project and achieve its goals. Therefore, I refused to substitute excellence for competence. Through ongoing dialog, we arrived at the following integration of our beliefs and mission:

 We believe that competence is an essential means of sustaining our values in a competitive marketplace.

Concurrently, the Mission Statement was changed to read:

 To value, contribute, and affirm a high level of commitment, skill, and effectiveness in the work community.

The board's editing committee accepted these changes. We had learned once again that living the Mission is an ongoing process. Like our nation's Constitution, the company's beliefs were able to adapt to market and business exigencies. As we lived in accordance with the Mission, we found that we had created a living, practical Mission.

DEFINING OUR DESTINY

We had ruffled some feathers, made some mistakes, and fired some employees, but in the end we stuck with the Mission, and soon it became part of the company's identity, how we saw ourselves and how other people saw us—a company that cared about its moral and social responsibilities as much as making a profit. Our new sense of what Jonathan Edwards had called "being as relation" was propelling Tom's forward to find our place in the competitive arena.

The Mission hasn't dulled our competitive edge or softened our will to win. Our concern for values and doing good hasn't made us too self-conscious, running a business as if we were standing outside it, checking every move for "political correctness." On the contrary, the triumph of the Mission—and its joy—is that we are being ourselves in running the business. Our knowledge that our values matter keeps reinforcing our identity, sharpening our competitive edge. Most important, we've taken control of our future. Thanks to the Mission, we have become the definers of our destiny. Believing in God doesn't mean that you must leave everything up to Him. Humans have an essential role to play in God's plan. As Martin Buber wrote in *I and Thou*,

 Destiny is not where we wait for God to push us. You know always in your heart that you need God . . . but do you not know, too, that God needs you—in the fullness of His eternity needs you? . . . The world is not divine sport. It is divine destiny. . . . We take part in creation, meet the Creator, reach out to Him, helpers and companions.

Finding a sense of identity for a company—its mission—is a journey through all kinds of uncertainty. It is a journey every company needs to try to take, so we can all

lead with who we are
live with who we are
progress according to who we are

But if our souls aren't on the journey, if our quest is only about figuring our economic worth, it will be just another strategy, just another plan, just another game. Living and working are too important to let that happen.

HOW TO IMPLEMENT A MISSION

1. Select a committee from the company leadership and rank and file. If the company is spread over several locations, create a committee for each. Be inclusive about the representation on the committee, but still make it accountable to the president.

2. Plan company events that focus initially on the objective of getting to know one another better. Traditional company recreations (picnics, outings, games) or fellowship events (retreats, assemblies, celebration breaks) usually can do the trick. Be sure the self-important executives attend.

3. Plan and design, with the help of human resource professionals, communications workshops, companywide. Let a few of the principles of the new mission statement be the focus of discussion. Be intentional about listening and sharing. Don't be defensive. Let the employees speak their mind, and record their feedback. To prove you were listening, make the results public—the good, the bad, and the ugly.

4. Have the committee work with leadership to assign the recommendations to appropriate groups for research and recommendations. Each group must keep the company aware of its progress.

5. Organize the list of recommendations into categories:

   • immediate action

   • deferred action until a certain date

   • no action planned at this time

6. Take action on simple things (like sprucing up the office, paving the parking lot, setting up a suggestion box) right away, to demonstrate your commitment to "live the mission."

7. Take time out to celebrate changes in the company that align with the spirit of the mission.

8. Reward people who are living the mission, where appropriate.

BUILDING
COMMUNITY:
THE POWER OF
STORYTELLING

Teamwork. How many times in your business career have you heard that term? How many times have you used it? It's the Holy Grail of American corporate life. Small companies often identify themselves as teams; large companies divide themselves into teams (such as the creative team, the executive team, the design team). But like many ideas that have been around for a long time, teamwork can mean different things to different business executives.

Too often what bosses mean by teamwork is that each worker on a team performs his or her job or function and each department does its thing—and never makes a mistake. But that's a team in the way that an assembly line is a team, which is really not a team at all but a human machine. One major difference between a company and a well-oiled machine is that one of the company's "parts" had a fight with his wife this morning; another wants her daughter to go to college but can't seem to save enough; another has had a death in the family. Thinking of a company as simply a collection of jobs being done so that profits can go to the bank turns the company into another version of Buber's "I-It" relationship. It dehumanizes employees, treats them as things, as mere job categories. It ignores their values, and above all, it ignores their stories.

As I have mentioned, at Tom's of Maine we believe in the value of listening. This ties into our belief in the power of *storytelling*. I don't mean telling dirty or ethnic jokes or teasing fellow workers, which is what too often passes for conversation in big business settings. I'm talking about telling a story that conveys who you are, that shares your values, that brings the people you work with into your life, that *identifies* you as more than a job category by informing the people around you of your joys as well as your problems.

An assembly line stops for no person's problems. I believe, however, that a company that operates on respect *has* to stop and moreover will, in the long run, benefit from the expression of such concern. That's why at Tom's of Maine we regularly take time out from the daily grind to celebrate human events and mourn the deaths or departures of our friends. It's why we encourage our workers *not* to work late or on weekends, but to go home and enjoy themselves and their families. Respecting other people is part of our Mission. Treating them as individuals and valued team members is too.

The essence of any company—its identity—is found in its beliefs, its values, and its stories. I think of a company as a community, a kind of extended family. Before you tell me that you've heard that one before, let me explain what I have in mind.

THE COMPANY AS COMMUNITY

When was the last time you had a conversation with one of your employees? I don't mean chitchat of the "Hot enough for you?" and "How 'bout those Celtics?" variety. I mean a real conversation where you actually learned something about the person's life. Typically, we bosses stroll down the corridors of power, nod to our employees, and that's that. Businesses have traditionally been organized into a hierarchy of positions that carry inherent power and authority, from the CEO to the mailroom. Jobs themselves are organized into different functions—marketing, sales, research and development, finance, manufacturing, service. The marketplace determines the relative value of a job. A person's worth is measured by the job he or she holds and how competent that he or she is. The job categories themselves can have their own hierarchy (for example, manufacturing is typically lower down on the pole than finance, and service might be perceived as lesser than marketing).

The bigger the company gets, the more rigidly these categories organize how human beings associate with one another. In a Fortune 500 company, a "lowly" worker in the mailroom or in a corner of the sales department might work until retirement without ever exchanging a word with the CEO. (Come to think of it, in the really large conglomerates, even relatively high-level executives might never talk to the big boss.) Within these various categories, there is also a "class system": worker, supervisor, middle managment, senior management, officers, and board of directors. When you examine the differences in education, social class, race, and gender in each of these classes of jobs, you tend to see that the American enterprise system provides the greatest opportunities for white males from Judeo-Christian families.

But many of us in corporate life also have another, very different kind of human association—the family. In the family we learn love, patience, respect, nurturing, affirmation, and health. The family also teaches us about competition, domination, selfishness, and deceit. The family is thus a relatively efficient learning system for the development of mind, spirit, and body. It involves the whole self. Certainly it has its own hierarchy and power centers, but it also can be egalitarian. Members of a happy, thriving family will do anything for each other; they devote themselves to maintaining that happiness and increasing it.

Substitute the word *company* for *family* in the previous paragraph, and you get an idea of what I envision a company community to include. In my experience, employees will run through walls for a company that understands them, gives them some freedom, encourages their creativity, appreciates their work, and rewards it fairly. Treat an employee like a cog in a machine, and you'll get a cog's work. Treat that same person as a member of your family, and you'll get eternal loyalty. A company does not exist without people, but people exist without the company—with their own lives to lead off the job. Any boss who ignores the stories they have to tell about their lives, their ups, their downs, their joys, their tragedies, is missing the chance to have relationships that will enrich him and his company as well.

We were lucky at Tom's of Maine and able to establish the feeling of an extended family because the company actually started as a family operation. In the early days, the company was just Kate and I. (Our third child was born during the first month we were in business.) When we created our first nonpolluting liquid detergent, Kate and our part-time secretary did the tests—on wash in their own machines. As the company grew, we were determined to keep our family culture. Now, with eighty-five employees, the Tom's of Maine family has grown into what Charlie over at the warehouse calls "more of a friendly village than a family."

At Tom's, as in any friendly village or happy family, people are not afraid to talk to each other. In fact, they depend on being able to. A few years ago, I was in a meeting with a top female executive in my company. Suddenly through the door burst another member of my executive committee with a wild look in his eyes. Before we could say a word, he announced that his wife's mother and sister had just been killed in an automobile accident. Before we could respond, he embraced me and began to cry. I held him until his sobbing subsided. Then he was ready to talk, and I simply listened. He talked of the difficulty of reconciling the fact that the night before these people had been in his house and today they were gone. He talked about how close his kids were to their grandmother and aunt, about his own love for them all, about his concern for his wife and her father. Coupled with his grief was his rage over evidence that their deaths had been caused by a car hurtling the wrong way down the turnpike—a drunk driver at the wheel.

He was having trouble making sense of it all, and since we

certainly couldn't either, we just listened. Once his emotion was spent, since we were members of the same church, I asked him if he wanted to pray. We joined hands in a circle, the three of us, and I said a few prayers that seemed to comfort him. Throughout the day I kept in touch with him and made sure everyone in the company knew about the funeral. My wife also talked to him, and we all went to the funeral. The day after the funeral, he showed up at work. He wanted to be in the company of the company. He needed our support. For this young executive Tom's of Maine had become like a family. He cared about the company because he knew the company cared about him—and not only because he had an MBA, or had turned down lucrative job offers to live in Maine, or was good at his job.

If you cannot imagine something like that ever happening in your own company, then you are missing one of the great joys of business life. I love watching sales go off the chart as much as the next CEO, but success is more than high numbers. I understand that a business requires a hierarchy, but I can't tell you how much satisfaction I get when certain bits of people's lives—the marriages, the births, the deaths, the loneliness, the addictions, the healing, the parenting—enter the life of the company and dissolve its power structure into a circle of mutual respect, support, and learning.

Our goal at Tom's of Maine is to respect the inherent dignity of each person as well as the job that person does. We want each employee to bring his or her whole self to work—values as well as job skills. Each of us performs *and* feels. In many companies, only one side of us takes on the challenge of doing the job to meet its goals (sales, production, or profit); the other side is put on hold, wanting to share its pain, confusion, or joy with others. At Tom's of Maine we want to see both sides of every person working together; we want to know one another as warehouse worker/father/husband; as vice-president/wife/mother/citizen.

In honoring the whole person we have chosen to form a community that is both hierarchical and egalitarian. We want to compete in the marketplace, but we think we can compete better from a foundation of humanness, from shared values. A community, we think, provides the fertile soil that will help us grow, reaching, like Jack's beanstalk, into the sky for more and more market share.

63

HOW I LEARNED
THE POWER OF STORYTELLING

A few years out of college, I landed a job at Aetna as an insurance salesman, one of nine working out of the Philadelphia office. There were three secretaries, one for each group of three salesmen. My group's secretary was a woman in her fifties named Virginia. The drill at the office was that Virginia began typing up the paperwork for the top guy and worked her way down the list, to me. Intensely ambitious, I knew immediately that this was going to be a problem. My goal was to see that Virginia did my work first and best, even though I was low man on the totem pole.

I achieved that goal within a few weeks. How? Well, first of all I had one major thing going for me: A senior salesman in my group was a real demanding autocrat. He made Virginia's life hell. My second secret weapon: My mother's name was also Virginia. Virginia soon began treating me as a kind of son, a young man that she was definitely going to train. Virginia had her share of problems, and I listened to her, often for a long time. I was hardly in a position to straighten out her life, but I at least paid attention to her; I treated her as a person. I hasten to add that this was hardly a chore. A babe in the woods of big business, I had a lot to learn. Virginia had spent most of her life working in offices, and she had plenty of wisdom to pass along. I listened, and she appreciated it—and she typed up my work first.

Young executives thrive on power and its perks. But nothing is more absurd in the business world—or more charged with potential for resentment—than a young man pulling rank on someone thirty years his senior who has forgotten more about the business than this kid knows. Virginia gave me my first lesson in how someone below me in the corporate hierarchy could make the boss look good. Happily, I was smart enough to recognize the converse: A vengeful underling can also make the boss look bad. Hierarchy is unavoidable in business. But I was lucky to learn from Virginia early in my career that the best work is often done when the importance of titles and job categories is ignored and a person's talents are respected. The best way to get beyond titles and the intimidating factor of corporate hierarchies is to trade stories with the people you work with.

DAILY STORYTELLING:
EVERYDAY COMMUNITY

Most families have a hierarchy, where parents are in charge and the older kids have more authority than their younger siblings. In those lucky families that have grandparents around a lot, the parents of parents can play the "wise adviser" role—another level in the hierarchy. Even in the looser, less "businesslike" atmosphere of a family, everyone knows who's in charge, everyone has a job to do, and they can get it done with love and for the good of the family, their *common* good. While certain figures in any family are "in power," a certain kind of equality can operate simultaneously. In this sense children as well as parents are equal as family members, as loving—and beloved—members of this small social unit who are all in it together.

One day at Tom's I saw a familiar form on my secretary's desk, an application for a college tuition plan. "That's the one we use," I told her. Joan looked at me for a moment, and I could see the boss-secretary relationship melt into an understanding between two parents about the financial burden these days of sending kids to college. Of course Joan knows I have debts, because when they chase me, they chase her. But I doubt she had ever considered that her boss had to borrow money to send his own kids to school. (I've sent three through private school and college, with one about to graduate from boarding school and begin college, and little Luke to go.) It was a new connection between us, a nice leveler. Joan has one daughter, I have two, one of them about the same age as Joan's. When Joan learns that I suddenly have to drive six hours to deal with a family problem and that she has to rearrange my schedule so I can get to my daughter's school, she just smiles and says, "Aren't children wonderful?"

I remember several years ago dropping off Luke at nursery

school. I was running late, and Luke wasn't in the best of moods. As I was helping him get his boots off, I looked up and saw someone I recognized but didn't expect to see in that context. I realized it was Ronda, who is in charge of answering consumer mail at Tom's of Maine. She, too, had been trying to get her son settled and then get to work when she saw me. At first I detected the mild discomfort that a staffer feels when running into the big boss. But then there we were, just two parents tidying up their sons' cubbies at the local nursery school. We said hello, and that was about it.

It was a small moment, but it changed our relationship. It gave boss and employee some common ground from which to operate. (All men and women are equal, especially to five-year-olds.) Now when Ronda and I meet, she asks about my family, and I hers. Because of "the family connection," when Ronda wants to make a point during staff discussion about consumer response, she feels free to pipe up because she knows that at least on one level—family—I share her concerns as a parent.

Ronda also knows that serving the customer fully and honestly is central to our philosophy of business. At Tom's we want people to talk to us, and that definitely includes our customers. One prime source of our self-education through storytelling has been listening to our customers. Each month, we get about one thousand letters, and we answer each one. Our customers let us know that they feel they're dealing with a company that listens, with real human beings (though many wonder, "Is Tom real?").

Ronda is in charge of dealing with Tom's of Maine's customers. For Ronda, communicating with customers is no mere job. "As long as I work in this company," she once told me, "there will never be a form letter sent to a consumer. *Never.*" She's not kidding. Her job—building the greater Tom's of Maine community through relationships with our customers—has become a passion, her mission. Ronda once told me, "Every letter gets answered as if it were a whole new important and single event, and everybody in my department knows that."

You can't fake that kind of commitment. And it's contagious. But would she feel that way about her job if she thought her bosses didn't give a damn about consumer mail, that it was some kind of public relations ploy, just eyewash?

Ronda's passion for her job comes from her clear knowledge of the company's mission and objectives—of its story. Storytelling inspires passion and creativity. A company that has lost its creativity and passion is a dying company. The thing that most terrified me when I was agonizing over what to do about my future—sell the company, study theology, or whatever—was that I had lost my passion for business. I did regain my passion and zeal for entrepreneurship through my work in divinity school, but I had to leave the company part time to do so.

I'd like to spare my employees that kind of anxiety. I want my company to engage their passions and creativity and channel that spirit into helping Tom's compete. I believe if I give them the freedom to grow, to experiment, to create, the company is bound to benefit, and so will they. They need the freedom to learn, which means making mistakes. As Katie Schisler confirmed for me, "No one has all the answers. We need to figure things out together through interdependence and learning from each other." And we do that through communicating, through telling stories.

Both Katie and Ronda feel free to throw themselves into their jobs because they know that the company wants them to, expects them to. Above all, they know that Kate and I are on their wavelength; we care about the company and its customers as much as they do. We have similar stories to tell about our families, about life at nursery school, about our favorite sports teams. If we think of each other only as "the boss," "the secretary," or "the guy in the warehouse," we are stripping each other of most of our humanity. Yes, I am the CEO, but I'm not only that. I'm a husband, a father, a sailor, and a student of theology, and within those alternative descriptions of me is plenty of common ground with the people I work with. Like the rest of the people working for Tom's of Maine, Kate and I are trying to bring both head and heart to work.

Those of us who build and run successful companies know that the future depends on stability. It is one of the simple paradoxes of business that companies will not grow successfully unless they are stable. They will not progress unless there is continuity. We need executives and line workers who are not only skilled but loyal to the company, who stay around long enough to pass their wisdom along to new or younger staffers. But unless an employee feels needed and respected, he or she is likely to grab the next best job offer. I've learned over and over that the best and easiest way for a boss to show his respect for his workers is to listen to them. This common effort enriches us all.

Daily exchanges like those with Ronda and Virginia—from the simplest kind of storytelling, the sharing of human kindness, respect, and concern, to active community-building among employees and customers—are sure ways of facilitating greater communication within a company. Other types of storytelling and building human connections are slightly different and represent increasingly deeper levels of active commitment to building community in a company.

CONSCIOUS COMMUNITY-BUILDING:
THE PROFITS OF MUTUAL RESPECT

No matter how much we might try, we can never head for the office and leave "the personal" at home. Expecting employees to do this is about as absurd as demanding that they be at their desks at nine—but leave their heads at home. Our personal and business selves are intertwined necessarily and inevitably. Both men and women are constantly juggling the personal and the professional, but caught up in their own busy schedules, they often forget how the personal side of their lives insinuates itself into their work.

One day, in the midst of trying to run the company and finish writing this book, I charged out of my office, probably on my way to the bathroom, when I passed Susan, an assistant to my vice-president of community life, Colleen. I said, as we all do, "How are you today?" I expected a "Fine, and you?" and maybe a smile, and I'd be on my way. But there was no smile. Susan simply said, "Oh, I'm just barely keeping it together." That certainly grabbed me. She continued, "I don't know whether I can hold together two more weeks."

I quickly forgot about where I was going and asked her what she meant. She answered, "Well, I miss Jeff so much. I don't think I can take it any longer." "Oh?" I said, not knowing that Jeff, her husband, was in the navy and had been at sea for three months and wouldn't be back for three more weeks. "I think three and a half months is just plain torture," Susan said. "I just don't think I can go through this again." She went on to tell me about the difficulty of being separated from a loved one for so long and how they had to make do with letters and long telephone calls.

I asked whether she sought comfort among the wives of other sailors. "No," she said. "I have my mother—and Colleen. Colleen is a saint." I tried to sympathize with her, but the fact is that in my twenty-seven years of marriage, my wife and I haven't been apart for longer than two weeks. "March fifteenth," she said, "five-oh-eight at the Portland Airport—that's when Jeff is due." She had it counted down, right to the minute.

A few days later, I was out of town when I thought of Susan. I called her. Colleen picked up the phone and asked if she could help. I said, "No, I'd just like to talk to Susan." Susan came to the phone, a little nonplussed. I asked her how she was coping. "A little better today," she said. I told her I was thinking about her and hoping she was getting through the day all right. She told me that she had just written to her husband in Barcelona—her last letter before he headed home. We traded some lines about Barcelona, one of my favorite cities, and that was that. Not a big deal for me, but she was very grateful for the gesture. It was one of those personal moments that is possible during the workday. Loneliness is hard, and it helps if someone at the office notices.

When people who work together step beyond the niceties of office chitchat and indulge in some real conversation that allows them insight into each other's lives, it enriches the experience of going to work. Any boss who gives people a reason to love going to work is going to see results in productivity that he's going to love.

WHY STORYTELLING
WORKS IN BUILDING COMMUNITY

Storytellers and listeners benefit from stories in different ways. Each of us comes to a story—and away from it—with different experiences. Each of us focuses on different details. I don't even expect your story to be absolutely accurate historically, because I understand that you, the storyteller, have selected those parts of your story that mean the most to you, that move you the most. When that senior executive burst into my room to tell me his wife's mother and sister had been killed, he didn't tell me every single detail of the accident—certainly not in the way, say, that the police at the scene reported it. He focused on certain things: how much he himself would miss the two women, how it would affect his wife and his children who had seen so much of them, and how it would affect his father-in-law.

As I listened compassionately to his story, I focused my attention on certain details rather than others, recalling some broken parts of my own life, tragedies that I too never thought I would survive. I, too, had seen the consequences of alcoholism in people's lives and come to know it as a disease. For him, that drunk driver was an outlaw, and there was no tree high enough to hang him from. I saw the man as sick, as much a victim of his alcoholism as were those people he killed. Every story we hear can teach us something about our own lives. The connection is not in the details but in the overall meaning. You will see an event in one way, I in an altogether different way. What we learn from that experience will be just as different and enriching.

In one of my classes at Harvard Divinity School, Professor Elisabeth Schüssler-Fiorenza, a renowned feminist theologian, asked sixteen of us students to read the same miracle story in the Gospel According to Mark and write our impressions. She received sixteen entirely different accounts, just as she had suspected she would. She explained that each of us imagined the scene in Mark differently because we brought our own life experience to the story. The American philosopher Alfred North Whitehead called this interaction of experiences an "interpretation" based upon how our individual histories influence what we see in the moment. You and I can stand on the same hillside, if I can interpret Whitehead, and take in the same beautiful view. But you might focus on the variety of trees in your view; I might focus on the multiplicity of flowers.

The employees at Tom's of Maine come from all walks of life. Workers making $30,000 a year are bound to view things differently from executives who arrive at Tom's from a Fortune 500 company. What does the Mission mean to eighty-five different people? The only way I can find out is if I try to get to know those people, if I listen to their stories, which will reveal the symbols—the meaning—of their lives. Storytelling can be an effective teaching tool because learning is not limited to what goes on in your mind. It is also about sharing what you know with others, and they with you. We all have our own beliefs, but we cannot expect others to understand who we really are if we keep those beliefs to ourselves.

A company committed to ethics as well as profit needs to affirm that knowledge of ethics—what it is that we *ought* to do—comes not from a course in organizational behavior in business school (or from a "business ethics" course) but from the bonds formed in the family, the church, the schools, the neighborhoods, and self-help groups. As persons, we are in a web of beliefs, traditions, and religious and cultural values. But no one will understand us as persons if we keep our beliefs private. Nor can we expect anyone to change their mind about their values if we don't talk to them about why we believe differently from them. We change as persons when we take on different beliefs and values that we learn ought to be part of our lives. I recently participated in an ethics seminar at a church in a wealthy New England community about "the responsibility of the religious life." When the subject of our moral responsibility to AIDS victims came up, one of the participants, Sister Mary Hennessey, who works with AIDS victims in Boston, pointed out that a Christian is called upon to go to the persons in need and ask them, "What are you experiencing?" By affirming that they are real and important, she explained, "we have to be prepared to be changed." Her message is that in giving of ourselves, the irony is that we are likely to be changed and grow in ways we didn't expect.

The key is not staying where you are but going to where they are. Their story is likely to change you. A few years ago, we hired June, a person with a developmental disability from the Kennebunk area, to fill a cleaning job. One day after a new set of offices was opened, June came to me and said, "Tom, can I have one of those offices?" Caught off guard, I said I'd think about it. The next day she came back and said, "I want one of those offices." I told her that I was sorry I hadn't considered her request, but those offices were already committed to other employees. I asked her why she wanted an office. "I have no place of my own," she replied. My reply: "Let's find you a place." June and I wandered around the office area until I noticed an out-of-the-way corner of a wide hallway. I set up a coat rack and a table with drawers and a lamp. June loved her new "office." What did I learn from this story? We all need a place of our own. If you open yourself to share with another and go to where they are, as Sister Mary said, "be prepared to be changed."

The Mission Statement at Tom's—the story of who we are and where we are going—has become a major force for change in the company because it has helped alter the way our employees perceive business. Typically, young executives arrive at a company eager to apply all the ideas and techniques they learned in business school or on their previous job. Their goal is to change the company. But at Tom's of Maine we begin on the presumption that people don't know everything, that they might actually learn something from our fellow employees, no matter how low in the hierarchy they might be. The story we tell as a company is one of constant change and challenge. The employees most likely to succeed at Tom's are those willing to learn something new, willing to change.

While writing this book, I spent a week visiting employees in different areas of the company to find out how the Mission, which had been in place for three and a half years, had affected them. "This Mission has allowed me to be a whole person," said Katie Shisler. "I can now balance my personal values with my work values. I feel that I can work all day long and still be working on things that I believe in, and on top of that I can give something back to the community as well." She also noted the excitement of pioneering a whole new way of doing business in America. "In the classical business world of brand-marketing, Procter & Gamble wrote the book. But integrating the common good with profitability—*we're* writing the book." We hope that our stories will inspire others to try new ways of doing business.

PLANNED STORYTELLING
AND COMMUNITY-BUILDING

I'm still amazed at the things I learn about people's lives just by bumping into them in the corridors and consciously taking the time to talk to them. But sometimes you have to set the scene a bit more actively and establish ways and places that encourage people to open up.

A few years ago, I decided that I needed to form a smaller leadership team. Historically, our company's managers all had met regularly, but as my team of executives grew, I realized that limiting regular meetings to eight participants, including some of the newer members of the company, would be more effective for decision making and for accomplishing our agendas. These people had come to Tom's with such different backgrounds—a woman with a master's degree in divinity, a young man from a top business school, a man who had moved up the ranks from the manufacturing end of the company—that we would have to get to know one another better in order to become a good working unit. I wanted to have a monthly meeting, but I also wanted us to get away from the office.

We chose bed-and-breakfast places in various small and beautiful ports along the coast of Maine. We'd gather on the first evening for dinner, afterward sit around for some casual talk and storytelling, and then meet the whole next day and do our business. One evening, instead of just telling stories, we decided to make a game of it. We wrote down a series of "life categories" ("How I met my spouse," "The greatest challenge in my life," "My greatest failure," and so on) and tossed them into a hat. When it was your turn, you'd pick a category from the hat and tell your story. As we moved around the circle, our sense of closeness and unity was incredible. We laughed and laughed, we poked fun at each other, and we had a great time. Suddenly, these people were no longer vice-president of whatever, or the man from Gillette or the woman from the Union Theological Seminary. They were people telling their stories, recounting their great moments in life and their failures. It was a wonderful game, and we had just made it up.

But it was my strategy. My effort to open people up was hardly spontaneous, unlike the decision to make a game of it, a made-up thing. We were just as intentional about it as the identification of a target audience in a media campaign, just as careful as buying one kind of machine to make toothpaste rather than another. One of the best reasons to be intentional about finding ways to learn more about employees is that you send the message to the community that it has permission to be fully human at work.

THE GREATER COMPANY COMMUNITY

One simple way to inform your staff about who they work with is to write about them in a company newsletter, as many companies already do, or in the annual report. One of the most emotional forums for telling stories, in our experience at Tom's, is the company gathering—the picnic, the birthday party, the baby shower, the retirement party. At one gathering we formed a circle, beginning with people with the longest service at Tom's and proceeding to the most recent employees. It was fascinating to see who was there and to hear the old-timers speak of what it had been like almost two decades ago, like "the day Tom fired everybody." (The real story is that the day I bought our first truck and drove it to the plant to pick up a shipment that had to be delivered to Boston in order to get a check to make payroll the next day, my *three* employees greeted me. I told them that someone had to drive to Boston. They all refused: One guy didn't drive, one had never been out of Kennebunk, and the third said he couldn't that day. "Okay," said I, adding, "you're all fired." I made the delivery myself. The next morning my secretary told me that I had been rash in firing my entire staff. I agreed and proceeded to write notes to all three and deliver them to their homes. They returned to work the next morning—and into the annals of the myths of Tom's of Maine, filed under "the day Tom fired *everybody*.")

In his book *On Human Care,* Arthur Dyck, my ethics teacher at divinity school, pointed out how important it is for any community to know its past, its heritage. The past helps people know what their values are and how they evolved. Ritual and ceremony are ways people accomplish that. When someone retires, it is a sad as well as a happy experience. An old friend is moving on, but he or she will be replaced by a new person whom we hope will become a new friend. To honor retirees, Blaine Tewksbury, the company's first chemist who was with us for almost twenty years, traditionally created a large collage that always brilliantly caught the personality and style of the person retiring. (We took three parties to honor Blaine; Kate composed an ode to him, and we pitched in to make a book of collages.)

One of the most affecting moments in the history of Tom's was the death of Tad Dow, a Harvard graduate and environmentalist who was the plant manager. Tad had moved to Maine about the same time Kate and I did, and when we met him, he was traveling up and down the coast of Maine helping communities organize local environmental commissions. He was doing a lot of good and making no money at it. I asked him to join Tom's, and he signed on as my administrative assistant. He soon became plant manager, a job better suited to his engineering background, and he was great. Then he found out he was dying from cancer. Tad was fifty.

It was a slow and agonizing process. In spite of his chemotherapy sessions in Boston, Tad would try to get into work a couple of days a week. He told me that it meant a lot to him to keep getting back into the Tom's community. "It's more than just work for me," he said. When he finally had to go into the hospital, I visited him regularly. A few months before, a friend from church had died young of cancer, and I was so frightened by the idea of death that I had stayed away from him. I was not about to repeat that performance.

One day I showed up in Tad's hospital room with a gift, a collection of the poems of Emily Dickinson, and asked him if he wanted me to read him a few. He said fine, and I began reading, though I quickly sensed that the poetry wasn't registering with him. In between poems, Tad looked at me and asked, "Are you afraid of dying?" The question caught me off guard, but I recovered quickly by saying, "I think that's the question I'm supposed to ask you." He asked me again. "Yes," I said. "I don't want to die before I've done what I was put on earth to do." He seemed to accept that response, and then we talked about how we had used our time in life. As an avid and effective environmentalist, Tad had achieved important things along the coast of Maine.

I gave the eulogy at his funeral, which was packed with people from the company. I told them what an honor it had been for me to be with him during his final days. I had discovered gentleness in the self-assured rugged environmental activist we all had known. The disease had brought out a vulnerability and loving spirit that none of us at Tom's had really been aware of. "But you all know that the closure of that life was not one simple act," I told Tad's family, friends, and colleagues. "His life goes on and on." To prove it, I told them that Tom's had decided to name a piece of land we owned on the river after Tad and turn it into a natural preserve in the honor of this committed environmentalist who had lived, worked, and died among us. So just as Tad had given us so much pleasure as a friend and co-worker when he was alive, he would be able to provide a beautiful, natural retreat for us, even after his death.

EXTENDING THE COMMUNITY

From the very first package we designed for our natural toothpaste, we have included a message on the label—addressed to "Dear new customers and old friends"—that tells the Tom's of Maine story, about how Kate and I had wanted to use products for ourselves and our children that didn't include additives, dyes, and preservatives and had created our own. The label also says, "We learn from our customers. We listen to what they say and respond with intelligent alternatives."

That this direct approach was unusual did not bother us because we knew that our customers were hardly typical. People who shop in health food stores are avidly interested in the ingredients in what they buy. Since Kate and I are, too, we figured that if we wanted to know more about the product and the company who sold it, so would our customers. The seed of this open approach began on the very first products—Apple Shampoo, Coco Orange Soap, Skin Lotion, and Rosemary Creme Rinse. Paul Hawken, then president of Erewhon Trading Company in Boston, helped create the concept of Tom's and advised from the beginning to keep our package straightforward and informational. It was a key, he reminded us, to keeping people better informed. The customer would know what to do from there.

Later, when we moved into supermarkets and drugstore chains where our customers would not be as passionate about ingredients or as well-informed about health matters, we knew the Tom's package would have to be even more educational. Check out a box of Crest, or some other mass-market toothpaste box, and you'll see that three of the four horizontal panels of the package are about brand identification, and the rest about information (ingredients, benefits, and the like). Tom's went in the opposite direction—three panels for information, one for brand identification.

We did that because customers in our focus groups indicate that they are eager to know about the company. Our test packages tell them what the ingredients are, their natural sources, and their purpose. They like that. But what they like even more, we have discovered to our amazement, is the part of the package in which we tell them the Tom's of Maine story. I had actually been a little embarrassed about addressing supermarket customers as "New customers and old friends" (the label on our products in health food stores says, "Dear brothers and sisters"). But it is precisely this intimacy that people in the focus groups love.

Our radio commercials, too, emphasize the personal. I myself tell the Tom's story and talk about the product. Customers prefer this to advertising slogans and jingles and a hard sell about product benefits. Another big hit is a radio commercial featuring my mother (my *real* mother, not some actress) telling the story about how as a kid I gave her a hard time about brushing my teeth because I hated the taste of those supersweet toothpastes.

Our focus group research shows that different people from different walks of life are bound to react differently to a product.

Giving them a story that they can relate to their own lives in their own different ways is likely to connect our company even to a diverse group of customers. I remember personally attending one focus group; the granola-eater with the long hair, I knew I could reach. But what about that ex-sailor with a pack of Camels rolled up in the sleeve of his T-shirt? Suddenly, he began talking about how important it is to reconnect with nature and saying he liked this product because it had natural ingredients. Amazing!

The individuality and diversity of our customers is reflected in their letters to us. My particular favorite correspondence style is when people just write on the inside of the package itself, put a stamp on it, and send it back to us. Basically, the letters begin, "I have never written to a company before, but I just wanted to say that we really like your product." They tell us that our toothpaste really cleans their teeth, that their kids love our brand of children's natural toothpaste (Outrageous Orange, and Silly Strawberry), and all the reasons why they're buying our products. The intimacy of the letters can be quite surprising. ("I was first introduced to your apple shampoo when I was in my girlfriend's shower," wrote one correspondent.)

SHARING OUR STORY WITH
THE COMMUNITY AT LARGE

If you've gotten this far in the book, you know that I believe that Tom's of Maine has something to teach other companies about injecting personal values into their business planning. That's my own mission, and I lose no opportunity to spread the good word. In the past few years, my wife and my vice-president of community life have also hit the speaking trail, explaining to community and business groups how companies can break free of the old-fashioned numbers game and prove that capitalism can have a human face, that businesses can profit from "I-Thou" relationships. As I write this, Kate has just shown me a speech she's giving in a few days to a work/family conference in Portland, Maine. The focus of her speech is on what

Tom's does to make sure our employees are able to balance their family and work life—generous insurance benefits for employees and their dependents, including a wellness checkup; 15 percent of employees on flex-time; subsidized child care; eldercare referral and education; parental leave for birth and adoption—for both men and women; and a compressed work week for our production employees. "Why do we do all this?" Kate asks in her speech. The answer: "We believe that both human beings and nature have inherent worth and deserve respect."

That's the first line in our Statement of Beliefs. Telling our story and listening to the stories of others is central to living up to our beliefs and mission at Tom's of Maine. Talking a good game, which we're very good at, is not enough. We're players too. What we are— our being—is always in relation to the people around us, including the community where our company resides. Christianity teaches us to "love thy neighbor." According to Arthur Dyck, that means do no harm, do good, and maintain a disposition to do good.

BUILDING A COMMUNITY:

MAKING THE STORY WORK

The key to getting people to tell their stories is creating opportunities for genuine conversation, then encouraging it. And listening to it. For your employees to open up, you can't be closed down. When I talk about the power of storytelling, I advise people to keep three things in mind—listen, reflect, share.

Here's a short list that can help your company discover the power of storytelling in building community and teams:

- The first level of storytelling is simple human expressions of concern. Stop in the hall and listen to someone who wants to share part of his or her life with you. Listen to the employee as a whole person. Listening and sharing help build identification with the company as a whole and protect its continuity as a community.

- The next level involves more deliberate action on your part. Plan celebrations of events of common living, such as birthdays, anniversaries, and retirements. Include families and friends in some company-sponsored recreational events.

- Good communications are key to the functioning of any company. The next level is to create systems that encourage dialogue in your organization and keep it going. Consumer letters and a company newsletter are great. The arrangement of offices can encourage interaction. The setup in an individual office is also crucial. The boss's desk can become a Berlin wall; I prefer a circle of chairs.

- Begin meetings by giving a brief "piece of you." This will signal that you are not one of those executives who discourage their employees from bringing their personal lives to work.

- Finally, extend the company identity to the community at large. Some Japanese company headquarters in American suburbs have done this by sponsoring cultural events or sports teams or by making donations to local schools and their activities. Some American companies have become active in sponsoring literacy and educational causes. If your company shows its caring for its geographical community, people will care about and support the company.

11

THE
QUEST FOR
GOODNESS

CO-CREATING AND
SELLING GOODNESS

I t is amazing what we achieved at Tom's of Maine within a few years of articulating our Mission. We were working to realize our vision of a company-as-community that could serve the industrialized world with natural, environmentally safe personal-care products. The board, executives, and employees had been converted to a commitment to manage for the common good as well as for profit. With a lot of conscious effort and enough controversy for any business, the Mission and the company had fused into one. Tom's of Maine *was* the Mission—"To be a profitable and successful company, while acting in a socially and environmentally responsible manner." We had achieved a revolution of sorts.

We had, in fact, *re-created* Tom's of Maine.

But we also had products to sell—twenty-three, to be exact. Our next challenge was to let consumers know more clearly than ever that Tom's is a different kind of company, one committed to the same values they are: excellence, quality, natural ingredients, protecting the environment, creativity, and social responsibility. In a word— *goodness*. Tom's of Maine isn't selling merely toothpaste or shampoo or deodorant. We are selling the idea of "the natural" and "the good." Our motive is not simply to make money but, in the process of making money, to do some good, for our employees, our customers, our community, and maybe even their community. It is important that consumers understand not only what separates Tom's products from other products on the shelves but what separates Tom's from those other companies. There is indeed an immense difference.

It's not as if we believe we have the patent on corporate virtue. You don't have to be in the "natural" business to do good. All you need is cash flow, and you can do a great deal of good in your own communities. The difference between Tom's and most companies is that we *choose* to do good; we look for opportunities. It is part of our nature, our identity.

But a few years ago we wondered how we could isolate that difference, distinguish it for the consumer, then sell it in the marketplace. We needed a clear marketing message about Tom's connection to goodness that could translate into a sixty-second TV commercial. Our experiences with advertising agencies, however, had always been disappointing; they never seemed to get what Tom's of Maine was about. We had limited our advertising to regional radio spots, done in-house with the help of a free-lance copywriter, typically featuring my voice telling the story of the founding of Tom's of Maine as a natural, personal-care family business.

After we formulated the Mission, however, we wanted to try something different so that our public advertising would reflect the changes in the company. But what would that be? And who could do the job?

Then the phone rang. "Hello, this is Ed McCabe," said a voice on the other end of the line. "I like your company. It's the sort of client I want to do business with." I knew McCabe's reputation as a brilliant maverick on Madison Avenue who created legendary advertising campaigns such as Perdue Chicken's "It takes a tough man to make a tender chicken" and Hebrew National's "We answer to a higher authority." I remembered reading somewhere that he had sold his company, dropped out, entered and finished the famous eight-thousand-mile Paris-Dakar Rallye auto race, only to return with a brand-new company. We made a lunch date in New York City, where McCabe explained to me, "I want my new business to be associated with products that are better for the world." I believed him. Here was a man who had been through stages in his life, who had been a huge success, a maverick, but was dissatisfied; he knew that life was about more than making money. I saw him as a man like myself. We made a deal.

IDENTIFYING AND
SELLING GOODNESS

After spending a few months learning about our business, the McCabe team created a concept for the campaign. We went to New York to hear their presentation. I reacted instantly—and emotionally: "We don't address our customers that way!" Their campaign did not work for me. While it focused on the need for customers to pay more attention to what was in the products they bought, it seemed to imply that the audience should know better. The tone was wrong. I wanted to grab the audience with a provocative message as much as McCabe did, but I didn't want Tom's of Maine to sound condescending. My marketing team was too infused with the Mission's commitment "to respect, value, and serve" our customers to allow that.

The Tom's of Maine position with its customers, I stressed to the McCabe team, needed to be one of coach, not judge. "You know that!" I told Ed McCabe. He had spent enough time with us, he had read our Mission Statement and discussed our beliefs. "You know that we don't judge our customers. We stand with them." Certainly, McCabe got my tone: I was talking deal-breaker.

McCabe stayed cool. He didn't think the campaign was judg-mental, but he understood what I meant and was still eager to come up with a way of satisfying us. The traditional route—for his team to go off on their own, create a single slogan, then try to sell us on it—was not going to work. His team and my team had to talk to each other. We assured him we did not want to write the campaign—we were in New York for his genius—but we wanted to be part of the process. "I promised that the campaign would reflect you," McCabe assured us. "We'll go back to work on it and stay in touch."

Two weeks later, he and his team returned with a new idea for the campaign called "Simple Wisdom." These words captured the key points McCabe wanted to use to sell Tom's of Maine products—made from pure and simple ingredients, manufactured in a part of the world that celebrates the simple life—while implying that using such products is a wise way to live. He intended to visit Maine people, he said, to capture their stories—a lobsterman, a boat-builder, a carpen-ter, a teacher—who would talk about their work and how it con-nected them to the natural wonders of Maine.

I had a slight tug in my gut about the word *wisdom*. It was a problem word for me; as a result of my theological studies, I did not belong to the philosophical camp that viewed "truth" and "knowl-edge" as already discovered and set in stone. My view was that we are still learning God's purpose in the world and that we discover our core values in day-to-day human struggle. For me, *wisdom* implies "we know." I didn't think we did. Again, as with McCabe's original idea, I didn't want my customers to think Tom's of Maine had access to some kind of divine knowledge or wisdom not within their own grasp. On the contrary, my view was that my customers and I were on the same journey to finding out how to live a worthy life.

But I didn't raise my objection because I felt foolish disagreeing a second time. I let the process move forward. We arranged for Ed and his team to spend a week in Maine meeting with Native Americans, carpenters, boat-builders, teachers, all of whom were my friends. These people shared their stories about how they've lived and what they have learned. The spots were produced, we okayed them, and they went on the air.

Two weeks into the campaign, I got a call from one of my directors, whose professional experience includes consumer packaged-goods advertising and marketing. "I don't believe 'Simple Wisdom' captures what Tom's of Maine is all about," he said. The nagging insecurity that I initially had became the sinking feeling that he was right. I told Ed McCabe that the campaign still failed to express who we were, and he was supremely annoyed, to say the least. "All of New York loves the ads," he said, assuring me that we'd sell tons of products.

"None of that matters," I replied. "You haven't found us. You promised that the ads would reflect who we are, and they don't. We've got to go back to the drawing board." It was a difficult moment for everyone.

I now knew that the Tom's of Maine creative team had to go back to the drawing board, before Ed's group got going again. It wasn't the McCabe team's fault that they hadn't captured the company in the ads if we ourselves couldn't convey our essence to them. It was a classic case of "fuzzy in, fuzzy out." We had to be clearer about our intentions. We had to figure out how to transform our beliefs and mission into an ad campaign about our products. I knew from experience that the core idea at Tom's was to create something *good*. What seemed to encapsulate everything that the company had always stood for as well as the reason people bought our products was—*goodness*. Tom's, as both the Mission and Beliefs statements articulate clearly, was about pursuing profit *and* goodness. That old line about the Quakers again came to mind: "By doing good, they did very well."

My Harvard studies came through for me again as I searched for a way for us to think more creatively about how to tell others about our commitment to goodness. We needed to unlock our identity, our beliefs, and our values in a way that would make it easier for the McCabe team to sell Tom's of Maine. I found the inspiration we needed in one of the most ancient stories about goodness and creation, the first chapter of the Book of Genesis. Here was the consummate story of goodness—the importance of calling it into existence, creating it, naming it, realizing it was good, and saying it was good, again and again. All the language and metaphors that are important to the creative process are in this archetypal story of bringing into being, and I wanted my marketing department and creative team to explore and understand them.

The verses of the first chapter of Genesis are filled with verbs about action and intention, about doing and willing the good:

> And God said, "Let there be light" . . . and the light was good. . . . And God said, "Let there be a firmament . . . let the waters be gathered . . . the dry land appear" . . . it was good. . . . And God said, "Let the earth put forth vegetation, plants yielding seed, and fruit trees bearing fruit. . . . Let there be lights . . . day . . . night . . . stars . . . evening . . . morning . . . let the waters bring forth living creatures. . . . the earth bring forth living creatures. . . . Let us make man in our image.". . . . And God saw everything that He had made, and, behold, it was very good.

For a day and a half, Kate and I, together with Katie Shisler and Colleen Myers, read to each other and thought out loud. Colleen read from T. S. Eliot's poem "The Hollow Men" about the "shadow" that falls between the idea and reality, between an impulse and a clear action—a notion that seemed to sum up our sense of confusion. Our goal was twofold: to develop a communications strategy that would unlock our identity, including our beliefs, values, and attitudes; and to identify the kind of customer we were working for.

I will admit that at first I was a little uncomfortable about sitting around reading the Bible and T. S. Eliot while one of the most creative admen in the history of Madison Avenue was waiting for some direction. What kind of a wimp turns to the Book of Genesis and blathers about "goodness" for almost two days when he's supposed to be defining his business strategy? I figured McCabe must be wondering how he got himself into business with such a bunch of nuts. I felt kind of foolish.

But who else but us could reflect on the company's identity to figure out what Tom's really wanted to achieve in the ads? We had to do it. We were the ones immersed in the unique business culture where values are merged into business strategy. How could we expect someone else to tell us what Tom's of Maine was and what the company's goals ought to be? We had a Statement of Beliefs and a Mission. Surely we could help the McCabe team transform that into a wonderful series of spots that would, in sixty seconds, turn someone who had never heard of Tom's of Maine into a believer—couldn't we?

At the end of a very productive working session, we came up with a list of objectives for a new communications strategy:

- to educate on product difference, company values, special interest projects

- to build with our customer a sense of *shared values,* common ground

- to convert customers to our products through awareness building, trial inducement, and reinforcement of repeat sales

- to affirm goodness in what we make, who we are, and in others

- to deliver a promise

- to connect our audience with nature

- to engage our audience in Tom's Mission as an extension of our shared values

- to empower our audience's autonomy

- to reflect our Mission in our communications

These were objectives the company could pursue in its advertising as well as promotions, sponsorships, public relations, personal selling, or any other way of conveying who we are and what Tom's is about. At the center of every one of these objectives was "goodness." We were creating a common good and were eager for others to join us in that quest. We took these results back to Ed McCabe.

McCabe's response was the classic reaction of most business people: Philosophy belongs in a public relations campaign, not in advertising. We argued that our own experience with our customers had indicated that they cared most about our dedication to natural products and the environment—in short, our company "philosophy."

Unconvinced, McCabe suggested we do some focus groups; he wanted to bring his case to the consumer.

What he heard from the consumer was what we had known all along: People in the focus groups said that the "Simple Wisdom" spots seemed to be more about the State of Maine than about Tom's. They wanted to know about our products, to become part of the decision-making process. Our point was made by these consumers, and they said it much better than we had.

With this information McCabe was ready to try again for a new campaign whose tone would be honest and straightforward. Its attitude had to be humble, invitational, respectful; it had to be about mutual goodness and building relations. The content of the spots, we had decided during our workshop, would affirm how the company was "co-creating goodness."

The McCabe team asked us to tell them more about what we meant by "co-creating goodness."

GENERATING A DIFFERENT
KIND OF GOODNESS

Traditionally, the business of American business has been the opposite of the Quaker maxim: Companies "do well" *rather than* "do good." Good deeds are what churches and other religious groups are supposed to do; doing good is the province of *nonprofit* companies and organizations that work in the community, devoting themselves to the needy or protecting the environment. Companies in business *for profit* are meant to devote themselves to calculating how to turn ideas, people, and material resources into financial gain. That's not to say they won't do some good in the process. Pharmaceutical firms invent new drugs that save lives, appliance makers create machines that save on drudgery around the home, automobiles give people a previously unimaginable freedom to travel, entrepreneurs create new products and thus new jobs.

Most businesses, however, do not *intend* to do good; it isn't their primary goal. At Tom's we are challenging the prevailing view that to "do good" is philanthropy's job, not business's. Jonathan Edwards had taught me that goodness was not something I could take for granted, that it would not just happen to me like clean air, warm sun, green trees, and blueberry pie after a delicious Maine lobster. Nor was goodness only a product attribute (a "good toothpaste," or milk from the local dairy that captured, its slogan said, "the natural goodness of Maine").

Edwards showed me that goodness—what he called benevolence—could be an action word. Benevolence, according to Edwards, is a demonstration of care and concern by one person for another. Benevolence is transmitted; it arises out of willing the good. (In fact, the word's Latin roots literally mean "willing the good.") It is in relation to other people that we find goodness. Wanting to be connected to those others is the energy that binds you to them and keeps you together. Our relationship with McCabe's team, for instance, hung together out of mutual respect. We believed in their talent, and I believed McCabe himself was serious when he told me at our first meeting that he wanted to do more than make money. We had what Edwards called consent—an affirmation of what we both believed in, the action of goodness.

Since we are humans, not God, we create goodness in partnership with others. At Tom's we see our partners in goodness as our customers; goodness is at the root of our relationship with the people who buy our products. They expect it of us. Like them, Tom's of Maine cares about people, nature, and communities. Goodness is not something "out there," standing still, like a rock, as most business leaders assume. Like invisible electric waves, goodness moves around us, but it has to be actively sought out and created. We have to choose to be part of it—we have to choose to be good. We can only do it in connection with others. That's what we meant when we told the McCabe team we wanted to be "co-creators in goodness."

The problem with the "Simple Wisdom" spot, we now realized, was that it closed the door on the very subject we were talking about. The commercial said Tom's was "simple" and "wise," when we really thought Tom's was not at all simple, nor did it have any lock on wisdom or "the Truth." "Simple Wisdom" presented Tom's message as a fait accompli, while we were really a company in motion, in process. Our message to our customers had always been: We have these natural products that we think you will appreciate and that will square with your own family values. Here they are, but let us know what you think. Thus we invited our customers into our own creative process; they become our "co-creators." We didn't pretend to have all the answers. Quite the contrary, as we admitted to the McCabe team, "There's real mystery in what we're talking about."

GOODNESS AS
PRODUCT DEVELOPMENT

Our ideas for new natural products have been intentional acts of doing good. On the face of it, some of the products were not *needed*. In certain cases, demographics and Nielsen ratings indicated that venturing out with these new products would be disastrous business decisions in a declining market. But Kate and I were convinced that our customers would recognize the goodness of our products, and we were right. We had a "good idea," we acted on it because we wanted to "do good" by the customers, and by doing good, we ended up making money.

Financial returns will follow good acts. How tired I grow in my struggle, year after year, to retrain young marketing professionals who come to Tom's with their "worldly" credentials to exploit rather than serve our relationship with the customer. Competition dominates their minds, blurring their ability to see the potential for a genuine relationship with the customer. The point of business is not to *trick* customers into buying your product, to manipulate them to your side rather than a competitor's. The goal of business should be to create a good product that will do well by the customers. The challenge of selling is to convince customers that your vision of the good coincides with their vision of the good. While there is an inherent sleaziness in trying to manipulate or trick customers, there is a real beauty in seeing your version of the good connect with the customers'.

Putting service to the customer ahead of beating your competitor to the punch is choosing beauty over the battle. If you can convince someone that your idea of what's good is his—a *natural toothpaste*, a deodorant that's not full of chemicals—then you don't have to worry about battling your competition. The customer will come over to your side without your even having to aim a shot at the competition.

GOODNESS AND CUSTOMERS

Put this question to your executives or employees: "Would you prefer to be isolated from your customers or connected to them?" How about this question: "Is it easier to develop a satisfying new product for customers with whom you have had no communication, or to invest in a product that has grown out of an active dialogue with your customers?" Brand loyalty, after all, is nothing but a *relationship* with customers who might end up using a product for the rest of their lives. So why is it that we're so blasé about something as important as brand loyalty, allowing it to be an accident, an unconscious habit? Shouldn't we set out from the beginning to establish this close relationship with our customers?

The answers to all the above questions are obvious. So why are we in business so enthralled by the numbers instead of trying to listen to what our customers really care about? The research may say that there aren't enough people out there to support a new product idea, but if you know your customers, if you have been in constant communication with them as neighbors, friends, and family for almost twenty years, you might well know that their reactions will defy the numbers. Simply choosing to move past analysis by quantitative research alone and to be in communication with customers is, by Jonathan Edwards's definition, good.

Ask a creative team: "What good would you like to do for your customers? Imagine them in the room with you while you discuss the merits of a product. Can you see their faces and hear their suggestions in your mind?" No businessperson in the midst of planning a second-rate product that she intends to sell for a first-rate price would ever want to have the customer in the room with her. If your executives can live with an invisible customer sitting in on their planning meetings, then they are the kind of management that takes relationship into account. That is commitment to service. That is good.

Customer relations have everything to do with a company's understanding of goodness. Frequently, marketers declare that "the customer is our chief concern" or "the customer is the only excuse for a business." But they don't always intend customers to be more than the means to a sale, a collection of deep pockets. Customers are worth a long-term relationship. Every executive should be willing to look a customer straight in the face and ask, "So what do you think of our product?" If she's afraid of what the customer might say, then she's not delivering on goodness.

GOODNESS AS FAITH

When Jonathan Edwards wrote that we must "consent" to goodness, he meant we must trust in it, persevere in it, believe that our own good intentions will be met with goodness in return—to have *faith* in the product and the customer. *Faith* is a word rarely used in the vocabulary of business. But it, too, has its place.

When our reformulated honeysuckle deodorant didn't work, we involved our customers in the reformulation of the product. If we hadn't known it before, we sure found out then that our customers have some real expectations of us. When we have used market-research focus groups, they have confirmed our shared sense of values with the company that goes beyond satisfaction or disappointment with one product's performance. "I think they are trying to make a healthy product for their customers and caring for their environment at the same time." Another said, "I like how they give me the facts about the ingredients and trust my judgment to decide if I want to try it. It feels as if they respect me." Another said, "I think Tom and Kate are two people trying to do the right thing for me and the environment. I feel good about them." They trust us to respect their intelligence and to make products with human goodness and the natural environment in mind.

We simply had to have faith in the good turning up. My creative team persevered in searching the globe for a vegetable-based propylene glycol that worked and that was in line with our value commitment to natural and environmentally safe ingredients. After hundreds of phone calls we discovered a new business that had been created for the sole purpose of producing glycols and alcohols from corn. "Do you really make propylene glycol from corn?" asked our company chemist. "Yes," the man on the other end of the phone answered, then added skeptically, "Do you really want some? We've just made our first forty thousand pounds." They couldn't believe it, nor could we. While problems with this solution remain—we find it necessary to invest in the technology to provide a continuous supply of stuff—persistence and faith have paid off, for us and for them. Thanks to their persistence in experimenting with corn for a renewable source of alcohol and glycol, we found the product that freed us of a petroleum-based ingredient in our otherwise-natural deodorant. After the embarrassing and costly recall, we are planning to go back to the market with a totally natural deodorant that works great. We just need to keep the faith.

As I think every businessman knows, and certainly every entrepreneur, sometimes all you have to hold on to is your faith in an idea or product or colleague. Implicit in our faith is that goodness is flowing all around us, and we're looking for ways to connect to its energy. This faith can often be the most powerful quality in a business relationship, yet few business leaders will admit to it, even during times of confusion, conflict, and failure, when faith is all they have going.

After the Tom's and McCabe creative teams' ideas missed twice, either side could have walked away. But I held us together by sheer faith that we could make it happen. I had faith in McCabe, and I also had faith in my products. I knew that Tom's had what every brand wants—a powerful idea. But I also knew that I didn't have the creative strategy to deliver that power to the audience. I needed a pro like McCabe to capture Tom's of Maine in a media campaign.

And he did.

"AND, BEHOLD, IT WAS VERY GOOD . . ."

You like to recycle, you like to read labels. Why are you using the same old toothpaste? What we make—a toothpaste with natural ingredients, with fluoride to clean teeth and prevent cavities—is as important as what we believe: that a company can be successful and responsible to the earth and its people. . . .

This was the McCabe team's new approach. When I saw it, my reaction was as immediate and strong as the last time, with one significant difference: This idea was right on target. Brilliant! When we took it to consumers in focus groups, their body language told the story, as well as their words: "You're right. Why haven't I changed my toothpaste? . . . You've given me more than one reason to try Tom's of Maine. I care about the same things Tom's of Maine does. . . . I appreciate the straightforward information with no hype. . . . You didn't tell me how to think or feel. . . . You're right, why am I using the same old toothpaste. I guess I just never thought about it."

Part of the brilliance of the McCabe concept was that for the first time in an advertisement, Tom's of Maine brought the Mission forward into the product sell. We talk about what we make and believe. In each spot, we've merged our values with information about the product. The response from focus groups has been amazing. The logic of "Why are you using the same toothpaste when you've changed the rest of your life?" hits them immediately—and hard. Their answer, typically: "You're right. I ought to change my toothpaste too."

The initial response to the McCabe media campaign has been a revelation. We used to think we had to work to educate the consumer about ingredients to convert him to our brand. But it turns out that the company's Mission—to respect people and nature—makes anyone who shares that goal into a customer wondering why he hasn't been using Tom's of Maine toothpaste. Customers care that the product is good, but they seem to care even more that the company is good.

I strongly believe that any businessperson who gives himself or herself over to the concept of goodness, makes it an integral part of his way of doing business and planning strategy, will not only create good products and a good relationship with his customers but will also run into goodness around every corner. It's too easy to get overwhelmed by the numbers, to think that profit and loss are all that counts. It almost happened to me and Tom's, but at divinity school I learned to stop and reflect about what really counts—our relationships with others, goodness, not just my private good or even my company's private good, but also the public good, the common good.

DOING GOOD IS WITHIN EVERY COMPANY'S GRASP

Even though *benevolence* is an old word for goodness, modern business might do well to reclaim it. Benevolence is more than making a deal; it's an attitude of being in relation, and a will to do something good. Do well; do good. Do both.

Can a retail store do well *and* do good? How about a bank, or an auto manufacturer, or a fertilizer plant, or a public utility? When I speak to audiences about goodness, inevitably someone raises his hand and says, "All this talk about values and goodness is fine for a company like Tom's of Maine. But I'm in wholesaling; the name of my company is insignificant to the consumer who only cares about the brands I sell. My business doesn't lend itself so easily to good deeds."

My answer: "How much do you want to bet?" If you have a cash flow, you can do good. Doing good is beyond the deal; it's tapping into the relation to the greater energy that the human spirit knows. Goodness is found in connecting spirits, relating to people's hearts and concerns. If you're a wholesaler of hardware goods, your heart undoubtedly cares about your community's economic health, about your environment, maybe about the quality of public education, and that's all you need to find a relation to other spirits. You don't need to know exactly what the project is; you just need to tell another businessperson that you care about helping. The force and energy of goodness will do the necessary connecting with other hearts to make something happen.

No matter how skeptical you are about the results, you only need to try once, and you'll become a believer. Goodness is infectious. In *The Gift*, poet and essayist Lewis Hyde writes, "We nourish the spirit by disbursing our gifts." For Hyde, to hold your rewards to yourself is to keep them out of circulation. What keeps the spirit of a gift nourished, he suggests, is "constant donation." Tom's of Maine is working at it.

DOING GOOD BY GIVING

At Tom's of Maine goodness is closely linked with giving. Doing good requires time, money, and people. It requires a commitment to building human relationships, not just building inventory. But that cost buys human motivation and valuable employee involvement in the workplace. Our tithing to support education, the arts, the environment, and human needs has included grants such as:

- A $10,000 donation to support public-access trails to the ocean to the Portland Shoreway Access Coalition.

- A $100,000 grant to the Harvard Divinity School for the creation of a Center of the Study of Values in Public Affairs to help create the needed dialogue about practical ethics among professors, clergy, business executives, and government leaders.

- A $15,000 grant to make up for cuts in state funding for Community Support Services, Inc., a local group we have worked with over the years. CSSI has helped hundreds of developmentally disabled individuals become independent citizens capable of contributing to the community. Tom's has hired some of the group's trainees. Our grants have inspired other local businesses to contribute to CSSI's shortfall.

Let me stress that these commitments are not hobbies for people at the top of the corporation, or private "feel-good" games. They are definitely not political. "It doesn't matter if you're a conservative or a liberal here," said an employee recently. "We each interact with the Mission, we interact with the community, and it makes you think of your own role in the community." These grants are companywide experiences in benevolence. Without exception, every employee at Tom's understands the experience of working with developmentally disabled people because we employ two of them. Our employees also get to hear and share with Native American friends of the company.

Benevolence is expected at Tom's, which is why we put our money where our values are by encouraging employees to donate five percent of their time at work—for which we still pay them their usual wages—to community needs. Our employees have worked in service to community nonprofit organizations, such as soup kitchens for the poor and homeless, mentoring programs for the young, and assisting nonprofits in planning and finances. The company chemist inspired many employees to work at the local soup kitchen. Our sales leader is a mentor in a local junior achievement program. Another employee has started a foundation for grants to hearing-impaired children. The list goes on and on.

That goodness is contagious at Tom's of Maine, we have found beyond any doubt. Such companywide experiences have not only connected us with our values and with each other, they have fed our souls. These joys and satisfactions, however, have come only because we *chose* to do good. Would we have given away so much money, or gotten involved in so many projects, or would our employees be devoting five percent of their time to good works, if Tom's of Maine hadn't made such giving a central part of its company identity and mission? I doubt it. Once you choose to do good, you will find it all around you and in every area of your business.

Our job as business leaders is to be open to the possibility of goodness, to find it unexpectedly, in places we wouldn't have guessed. That's part of the mystery of goodness, part of its divinity. Doing well is essential for any business; doing good is its real dividend. Do good, and the good will look out for you. We can, in fact, work at being good, being open, claiming it. But that's not always how goodness appears. Sometimes, it comes right out of the blue and is not always deserved. That's what theologians call "grace."

COUNTING MY BLESSINGS

Grace, this unexpected kind of good, has blessed every major success at Tom's of Maine. Kate and I have tried to do good, and good people keep popping up in our lives to help us make the task a whole lot easier. I don't think I'm exaggerating when I say that not one of the people who've helped me turn Tom's into a success did I choose in the sense of a rational, planned process. Business partners and board members as well as a series of "good hires" have always materialized out of nowhere. They have, in a sense, chosen me.

I met my co-founder, Dick Spencer, a consumer activist and attorney who was working for Ralph Nader in Maine, at my kids' new school, an alternative elementary school called the School Around Us that we helped found in the early 1970s. I told him about it, and he liked my idea for a new kind of personal-care-products company so much that he lent me money to get it off the ground. John Rockwell, one of my first board members, read about the company in a local newspaper on one of his weekend trips to Maine from New York. My chemist Blaine Tewksbury's car broke down outside our offices. I first met my chief financial officer, Chet Homer, when he was working for a big accounting company and auditing my books. We got into an argument about how many pounds of coconut oil were in the fifty-gallon drums in the parking lot. We disagreed, but I was impressed with his ability to get to the core of an issue. Ten years later, when my board was screaming for more control over company expenses, a friend informed me that Chet, who lived in Kennebunk, was doing consulting work on his own. We made a consulting deal, and six months later he joined the company.

Pearl Rutledge, the organizational psychologist who helped us learn to live our Mission, ran a training seminar at the American Management Association in New York State that I attended way back in 1979. In the summer of 1985, Pearl and her husband were vacationing in Maine and came by my house for a visit. It was an extraordinary coincidence. Pearl helped me to realize that I had deeply rooted questions about my role in life, and her visit was the turning point and the inspiration to start thinking about studying theology. Within a year I talked her into joining the board.

Katie Shisler, my marketing vice-president, wrote me a letter looking for a job. After our first meeting I was so impressed, I sent her to meet with John Rockwell. "Tell me what's wrong with her," I said. "I can't see it yet." Rockwell didn't see it, either, and over the past three years Katie's turned into one of my top people. While searching for someone to fill the new post of vice-president of community life, I was giving a speech in Portland. Afterward, Colleen Myers introduced herself to me as an attorney who had a master's of divinity degree from New York's Union Theological Seminary—just the kind of unusual professional combination that was perfect for my (unusual) new post. I hired her.

Ruth Purtilo, an ethics professor at Creighton University in Nebraska, visited Harvard Divinity School for a semester during my last year and taught a course called "Good Service, Good Business, and the Good Life." I wrote a paper for the course that she liked so much, she suggested I try to get it published. That paper has turned into this book. (Ruth joined the Tom's of Maine board in 1991.)

Perhaps the most amazing grace bestowed on me was the way I got Father Philip Allen, an Episcopal priest from Minneapolis, to join the board. I had been eager to find a Native American for the board, but not just a token. I wanted someone who could bring the values of Native people to Tom's, who could share the values of the company and still have the financial acumen to discuss salaries, incentives, and balance sheets. At the Triennial Convention of the Episcopal Church in Phoenix in 1991, I sat on an environmental subcommittee with Father Allen, who happens to be a Lakota Sioux. Our task was to draft proposed legislation for the Church's position on the environmental crisis. We stunned the committee by beefing up a draft of a minor piece of legislation and making our new points the focus of the legislation that eventually passed—committing the Episcopal Church for the first time ever to the environmental movement. It was a great triumph for two of the politically less powerful souls at that convention.

I invited Father Allen to join the board. He said he'd think about it, though he warned me that his Church duties and his Native American concerns did not leave him much time. Back in Maine, I mailed him a formal invitation. Over the next few weeks we tried to reach him by phone to get his answer, without any luck. One day, waiting for a plane at New York's LaGuardia Airport, I decided to call Father Allen one more time. I looked for a phone—and saw the same Father Allen sitting across the lobby, waiting for a plane to Minneapolis. He was just as surprised to see me as I was to see him. I asked him if he'd made up his mind. "I've been waiting for a sign to help me make a decision," he said. "Seeing you here is more than enough. I would love to be on your board, if you still want me."

Sometimes the good finds us—as long as we're willing to be found. That's not to say I've replaced analysis, market research, and executive recruiters with tarot cards. Remember, I'm not talking about something passive here. Goodness is an action, intentional. When I say goodness for me is a kind of grace, I'm not talking about some force that paves the way for me. It's a co-creative process. Recognizing the good and acting on it is a state of mind. Faith in the good simply widens the range of choices before us. Business leaders need to find the courage to manage with a flexibility that allows them to see the good around them and choose it. If we can create an environment in our companies where managers say, "I'm feeling something other than what is on paper," or "I'm not going to decide right now because I have faith that a good answer will present itself," we will contribute to the good we're seeking.

These are the kinds of comments business leaders whisper to themselves all the time. Say it out loud! Take on the skeptics; meet them head-on. Every business leader I know can point to decisions, choices, or moves he or she has made by going against the grain, by trusting instincts, by having faith. Listen for goodness, and look for its signs. Encourage it in the workplace.

WHY DO GOOD?

I have debated this question at length with a member of my board: "Do we do good for gain, or for its own sake?" I am convinced that what gives Tom's of Maine its competitive energy is the permission we give each other to do good for its own sake. But the company's consciousness of the good must be encouraged, expanded. Employees must be reminded that we as a company care about the good. If we don't allow work to be a place for contributing to the good and pat people on the back for their good works, goodness will languish or be compromised. (As in "Goodness is a priority around here, but we have a chance to make a killing, so let's just put our values on the back burner just this once.") Goodness that becomes an explicit business principle comes alive and stays alive.

If you asked your board members, "What specific good shall we focus on this fiscal year?" could they give you an answer? Could your managers or employees or customers come up with an answer to the same question? We actually put that question to our customers, and they told us they wanted to see real evidence of our concern for the environment. They urged us to reduce and recycle our packaging and to deal with waste responsibly. In response, we changed the packaging on our deodorant, using less paper.

Would you dare ask the community in which your company is located to tell you what they would like your company to do for them? I'll admit I've never asked that question. But I'm now giving it some thought. Imagine Tom's of Maine, or any company, posting this kind of notice or advertisement:

 The company will convene a public meeting to hear what residents would like our company to do to help the community.

I suspect that the results would be quite amazing—and good.

MAKING GOODNESS HAPPEN

Goodness is not achieved passively. It requires an active commitment. You first need to "will the good." And you have to be willing to implement the good in ways that are not just window-dressing or corporate public relations.

1. To create goodness and make it part of the company community:

   • Listen to others. Prepare yourself to see goodness around you. Let others know when they have helped construct goodness; celebrate and affirm it when it happens.

   • Be clear in the company's commitment to making goodness happen. Help your employees to focus on goodness as a goal in their ideas and projects.

   • Be light-handed with the process. Goodness is co-created, not controlled. If you attempt to control it, you separate yourself from it. Goodness is in connection, not isolation.

2. Clarify your company's mission: does it articulate your commitment to creating goodness? Identify where goodness happens in your company, whether it's inside the community, in a product, or in relations with customers, and take steps to make its creation more purposeful. How can goodness be created in all areas of the company? Identify where it is being created and how and why, and electrify other parts of the company with it.

3. Actively give to your community. Ask your employees what the company can do—and how it can do it—to co-create goodness in the community. Listen to the ways they personally would like to give—whether in time or talent or specific activities. Encourage them to think of gift-giving as a continuous process, not a one-time decision.

6

INSPIRING
AND MANAGING
CREATIVITY

A t the beginning of any project, you can't control every variable. One thing I've learned from living in Maine all these years is that using a creative approach to problem solving in business is like navigating at sea. Sailing along the coast of Maine in our yawl *Intuition*, in and out of picturesque harbors and among islands, I've learned that you have to turn over some control to nature. You have to learn to read the wind and the tide, consider your options, and go with them. Whatever path you've plotted, the shifting wind along with the direction and seep of the tide will resist your course and force you to correct your bearings. That yawl has a feel for where it's going.

So it is in life, and business; you must find your way by trial and error, by intuitive response to uncertainty. Executives who can't understand someone else's intuition are like people sitting in a powerboat wondering why that sailing yawl has suddenly tacked in a different direction.

Each of us tries to chart a course in a vast system of interrelationships. In the uncertainty of it all, the right course is usually revealed to us as we make our way in the midst of the opposing forces arrayed around us. I've learned to find the intuitive gift in myself and in others, to get that vision shared so that others can build up on it or edit it, plot the right strategy, and get on with the job. Editing as you go is part of the process of gaining more and more intimacy with the creative unfolding of an idea. A management team is in constant motion, feeling and analyzing our way through interconnected, changing forces.

Kate and I have always thrived on developing new health care products out of our intuitions. We've been blessed with creative natures and are fortunate to have built our own business through which to express them. We've tried to make Tom's of Maine an environment conducive to expressing the creativity of all our employees, in all aspects of their jobs. Since the Mission re-created us, Tom's of Maine has launched four new products, and a whole new exciting line of products is in the works. Keeping the creative energy of any company from being hampered by overanalysis and skepticism, however, is a battle all businesspeople share.

In 1988, Kate and I decided to develop a children's toothpaste, something we knew our customers would want for their kids. We presented the idea to our sales and marketing executives. "It's not a growth category," they said, pointing to the infamous research and demographics numbers showing that the market for children's toothpaste was declining. Our key, front-line executives advised against going ahead with the new product.

But Kate and I argued that if parents had a choice, they wouldn't split their values and buy a natural toothpaste for themselves and a sweet brand packed with synthetic ingredients for their children. How did we "know" that? We certainly didn't have any scientific studies to refer to, and the numbers, as our managers had pointed out, contradicted our position. In fact, neither Kate nor I was banking our idea on any hard evidence at all. We simply felt that our toothpaste customers would buy a natural toothpaste for their kids because Kate and I would buy a natural brand for our own children, if it were available.

The question of "markets" has never driven Tom's of Maine. We create products by identifying with the families who buy our products. At the core of this identification are these values we share and a desire for "goodness," for quality, for connection.

Our creative successes have been all about *intuition*. We have had a feel for what people think is good and what will meet that standard. Relying on our intuition and identification with our consumers gives us a very special relationship with the customer, a kind of intimacy. As in any special relationship, when you feel a bond with the other person, you want to imagine what it's like to be in their shoes. You want to feel their situation.

That's what Kate and I were doing with our children's brand. We knew why we had a passion for the idea—a natural fruit flavor made for a child's palate, no blue dyes, starbursts, or supersweet saccharin, no preservatives, none of the junk—even if we couldn't justify the integrity of the product by the numbers. We held our ground, Kate went ahead and developed a children's toothpaste, we shipped it, and it was an instant hit. Incredibly, 90 percent of our store accounts added Tom's Outrageous Orange and Silly Strawberry to their shelves, next to our adult toothpaste brands.

For Kate and me, this most recent product success is only more proof that every businessperson must trust his or her instincts. While intuitions may arise in us mysteriously, the creativity necessary to make an idea happen, I believe, is something we can inspire and encourage in ourselves and others to accomplish our goals. Entrepreneurs live and die by their intuitions and creativity. I had even retreated from full-time business to part-time divinity school because I had had an intuition that I was, ironically, no longer following my intuitions. But once I had gained the moral arguments that came from my studies' validation of my sense that I *could* run a business without abandoning my values, I was able to return to Kennebunk and do the most creative thing I've ever done in business—re-create Tom's of Maine.

WHAT IS INTUITION?

There are various definitions of *intuition,* but for me, intuition is one of those moments when a light bulb turns on in your brain. Instantly. It's an idea that may or may not be the end of some long process of intensive thinking or logical discussion. It sometimes simply drops into your mind, in a moment, and is absolutely, positively self-evident. Other times, intuition is more like a leaning toward another place, a draw, a pull, or a push sending you in another direction changing your course.

An intuition is not a fantasy or a whim. A true intuition makes sense; it has its own logic. It's that ability to know somehow that there's a valley on the other side of the horizon, and that what lies in that valley is a good reason for making the journey there. In my opinion, intuition is something outside time and space. It is my connection to the greater human spirit, the collective consciousness of the human species—my bond, if you will, to God.

When I have an intuition, it's as if I have an invisible partner working on my behalf, feeding me an idea. In that sense, I view my ability for intuition as a gift not unlike perfect pitch for a musician, or the mathematician's talent for looking at a blackboard full of num-bers and seeing a beautiful formula, or a great outfielder's sense of where to run and leap to catch the ball before it flies over the fence. Not everyone in business knows they have a capacity for intuition—which is why those of us who use this gift must fight for our brain-storms.

The children's toothpaste packaging envisioned by Kate, our marketing staff, and our graphics designer Rod was unlike anything that had ever appeared on a Tom's product—fruits and animals in a rain forest. As soon as Kate and I saw it, we were delighted by the creativity of the illustration. Then the marketing department, in spite of having been part of the initial design meeting, weighed in with its reaction: The product benefit isn't clear, design not serious enough for a toothpaste, changes necessary.

I intervened and suggested they listen to Rod's story of how he had come up with the rainforest animals motif. The more we all listened to Rod talking about how much his own grandchildren love animals and fruits, how they enjoy interacting with fictional characters, the more Rod brought us into the mind of a four-year old, the more we realized we had to get our heads out of the Nielsen ratings and away from the utilitarian view that the only thing on the package that counts is the list of product benefits. I left the marketing department with a simple message: "Let the designer's vision unfold fully; don't overanalyze what this product should be; don't mess with this creative gift. Encourage him to say more about what he feels or sees."

Thereafter, "the world of a child" began to take over the whole product concept. We didn't need to license a character from *Sesame Street* or Richard Scarry, the popular illustrator of children's books. We had created our own characters. Before we knew it, the marketing department had joined in the spirit and begun working with the National Wildlife Foundation to do a joint promotion with our new kids' toothpaste and their *Ranger Rick* children's magazine. They also drew my nine-year-old son Luke into the overall communications strategy. The package included a letter from Luke in which he shares the names of his dogs, bird, and hamster. He invites other children to write and tell him about their pets. In response, Taylor, age seven, sent pictures of his three fish, his snail named Spike, and his cat, Leo, and said, "We like your toothpaste." Another child, Justin, wrote, "I like the flavor because it doesn't sting my mouth." These kids' reactions prove that the project had stayed on a creative, honest level; a good-sense strategy had made it happen.

Most entrepreneurs will admit to the power of certain insights they had at critical moments in their business careers. If the ego is willing to listen, it will hear, and the important messages will always come from outside of us. I didn't always know that. But it became clear to me when I realized that if I had ignored my intuitions, I would still be selling insurance, and not very happily.

BUILDING TOM'S OF MAINE
BY INTUITION

Whatever success I've had in business has often been due to following my intuitions. In 1968, twenty years before our struggle over the children's toothpaste idea, I stood in an elevator in the Aetna Casualty and Life Insurance building in Philadelphia, the hottest young salesman in the office and the only one who didn't wear a hat. In those days, years after John F. Kennedy's hatless style had destroyed the headware business, Aetna agents still sported headwear—hats with narrow little brims, like Bethlehem Steel helmets. One morning, the regional manager stepped onto the elevator and greeted me in his gruff voice, "When are you going to get a hat?"

"Oh, I'm considering it," I replied, and went downtown and bought a hat—with a wide, rakish brim, a hat worthy of Frank Sinatra. I had my hat, but I also had this feeling that I had better find a career where I had a little more room for self-expression. I began thinking about the open spaces, the beauty, and the special people of Maine, where my family had vacationed since I was a child. I had this feeling that I wanted not only a better life for my family outside the city, but to find my own way, to pioneer in business. So we moved to southern Maine to work with my father, an entrepreneur who had taught me to trust my instincts and to live with risks. After helping him for two years with his business, manufacturing industrial detergents, I was ready to branch off on my own.

I had this idea for a detergent that could clean the stainless-steel equipment used in dairies but without the phosphates that pollute rivers and water tables. No such detergent existed, but I didn't see any reason why I couldn't find a chemist who would help me invent one. I did, and within a year our friends were asking if the detergent could work on clothes. With some modifications, we developed Clearlake, the first liquid nonpolluting laundry detergent in the nation. (Clearlake was packaged in a plastic container that could be returned to us by a U.S. Postal Business Reply—and thus was a nonpolluting cleaner in a returnable container in 1971!) Two amateurs in their twenties, Kate and I were suddenly in business, up against Procter & Gamble and Lever Brothers.

But we were hardly alone. We were meeting people like ourselves, with similar values about community and the environment. We started an alternative elementary school for our kids. I discussed my ideas for the company with another founder of the school, Dick Spencer, who ended up loaning us $5,000 to get the company off the ground. Paul Hawken of Erewhon Foods liked our pollution-free laundry detergent so much, he suggested we develop a line of hair and skin products to be sold in natural food stores. With Paul's generous help and advice, we educated ourselves about the people who shopped in health food stores and were struck by our shared values. If the food we ate was organic or free of synthetics, why should our soap be a bar of chemicals? We hired a chemist, the one whose car broke down outside my part-time secretary's office in Kennebunk. We called our company Tom's Natural Soaps and developed and sold Apple Shampoo, Rosemary Creme Rinse, Pure Plant Lotion, and Coco Orange Soap.

In 1975 I had another idea—a natural toothpaste. "You know what's in toothpaste?" I said to Kate one evening, reeling off the ingredients: carboxymethyl cellulose, trisodium phosphate, saccharin, methyl paraben, and FD&C reds and blues. Kate was reluctant to get involved with what people put into their mouths. "I don't agree," I said to her. I wanted to make a product that was totally different from anything on the market, all natural. Tom's of Maine natural toothpaste was an instant hit from day one and soon became our number-one product—despite what everyone had said. The toothpaste made the company.

"How about a natural deodorant?" I then wondered. Take a look at a major brand deodorant; it's like a small chemical factory. Again, the nay-sayers worried about the risks of entering a new area. What if the deodorant caused a rash—there would be complaints, liabilities, and lawsuits. "We'll figure it out," I said, and in spite of some major obstacles and disappointments along the way, we finally did figure it out.

Had I listened to my advisers and friends (even Kate had initial reservations about these products), we would never have created the products that turned Tom's of Maine, as the company was renamed in 1981, into a competitive presence on the shelves. I persevered because on the other side of the horizon I could envision my company becoming the leader in natural personal-care products; I saw Tom's of Maine as the Procter & Gamble for young people who wanted natural shampoos, deodorants, toothpaste, mouthwashes, lotions—you name it. If it could be made naturally and still do the job, I wanted to make it and sell it.

My father the entrepreneur had taught me to follow my intuitions, damn the risks. He had created one company that failed, picked himself up, and created another company that was a long-term success. As I'd learned from him, entrepreneurs cannot be afraid of failing. They just have to be prepared to face the consequences. Nor can they be cowed by "the research" and "the numbers" because entrepreneurship by definition is creating something *new,* discovering markets that no one ever thought were there, markets that will not be counted until the entrepreneur announces they are there. That is not to say that the entrepreneur never pays attention to research or surveys, but when he looks at the numbers he is likely to see something that the bean-counters never noticed.

In 1978 I decided we needed a brand of fluoride toothpaste. Our research showed that only 40 percent of the people who shopped in health food stores were buying nonfluoridated toothpaste. That meant the other 60 percent were buying fluoride brands at the drugstore or supermarket. They were our customers, and I wanted them. My marketing department gulped: Fluoride remained controversial among natural food enthusiasts, and some health food stores would definitely throw us out. My executives wanted to leave well enough alone, but I wanted to give my customers the choice of fluoride.

Within two years the sales of our fluoride toothpaste began to outstrip sales of the regular toothpaste. By taking a chance on the natural fluoride brand, we had *more than doubled* our toothpaste business. Tom's bucked the conventional wisdom once again in 1986 with Kate's idea for the baking soda toothpaste. Another hit.

Yet again, in the 1990s, I was fighting the same battle—our intuition versus the utility of the idea—over our latest brainstorm, the children's toothpaste. But with the help of my theological studies and the Mission, I finally recognized that you should never allow analysis to elbow intuition out of the way without a fight. The genius of the Mission was in opening up the imaginations of all of us to the new possibilities in managing both for profit and for the common good. Then the creativity at Tom's just flowed.

THE RE-CREATIVE IMAGINATION

Recently, some friends of my twenty-one-year-old daughter Sarah were visiting with us in Kennebunk. Sarah later told us that during their stay her friends had remarked, "Your parents are very different from each other." Sarah's friends were right, and the differences between Kate and me are evident in the history of Tom's of Maine. Kate is the artist of the family, the poet, the chef, the gardener, and somehow she's managed to blend and fuse her talents with me, the visionary, the promoter, the salesman, the organizer, the hard-driver. We often see the world—and business—very differently.

Not long ago, Kate suggested that Tom's open a retail store, a factory outlet. I opposed the idea, pointing out that we didn't have time to dedicate company resources to retailing; besides, we had a different distribution strategy. But Kate stuck to her intuition that an outlet store would be another good way to serve our customers while promoting the Tom's of Maine name. She went to work. This year, the outlet we run in Kennebunk will do over a quarter of a million dollars in business.

We are people of contrast who still manage to come together and create one very good company. In divinity school I discovered that this kind of creative interaction between opposites has a venerable pedigree. Samuel Taylor Coleridge, the nineteenth-century British poet, called it the "philosophic imagination." For Coleridge, the author of "Kubla Khan" and "The Rime of the Ancient Mariner," this kind of imagination was not the staring-out-of-windows variety, or a kind of fancy; nor does it comprise mental associations from prior experiences. Coleridge viewed philosophic imagination as a "sacred power" by which two entities, often in opposition, interact with each other and fuse into one.

The creative process, the process of imagination, happens when these two contrasting forces come together, each with its own integrity, but each able to give way to the other to form something new. I, for instance, want to pursue the company's Mission as a marketer of wonderful natural personal-care products; Kate suggests a retail outlet. Both aims seem incompatible at first, until we discover that the outlet not only furthers *my* goals for Tom's but also achieves Kate's vision, while giving an unexpected boost to our profits. Our two views fuse together, without destroying their integrity, to make something new that preserves and enhances the company's identity. A creative re-creation. Imagination, for Coleridge, is "a vital, dynamic, sacred force." It has a regenerative and refreshing power. "It dissolves, defuses, dissipates, in order to recreate," wrote Coleridge.

A similar kind of "re-creation" has taken place at Tom's of Maine during the past three years. Let me explain what I mean by this creative re-creation, because it's at the center of my ideas about what it takes to make an innovative, socially responsible, and profitable company.

The Rational and the Creative: A Powerful Synergy

The Mission Statement implies that Tom's doesn't have to be all analysis or all intuition. It can be both. We can have it all—a company that encourages the two sides of every businessperson, the hard-nosed rational pursuit for more profits with the creative spirit for how to realize them. We can have a company that integrates the profit motive with the urge to do something for the community at large.

"But I've never had a brilliant breakthrough idea," some of you might say. "That light bulb of intuition has never popped on in my head. I'm a nuts-and-bolts, bottom-line kind of businessperson—and proud of it." This doesn't mean you can't manage creatively. I believe that any smart businessperson can manage creatively, if he's willing to take some risks and encourage creativity in his executives and employees. Building a values-oriented company like Tom's of Maine is a trial-and-error process. Succeeding in the face of risks gives you the confidence to take another chance today.

Currently, I'm working with my market development team, which consists of my sales and marketing leadership, to envision what the full potential would be of an integrated line of our many products. "Forget the historical view, and tell me what you imagine the upside market share is for our toothpastes, our deodorants, our other products," I've told them. "Talk over among yourselves what you think is possible. Let that vision anchor your strategy. Let's all agree on our goals—ten percent of toothpaste, five percent of deodorant, and so on."

No one among them, at this point in our Mission, would dare to pull out the Nielsen trends in my presence. I want them to live on quicksand, to feel awkward, to speak their suppressed hopes. I want to hear their dreams for these products and for the company before I hear their rational analysis. We have no foundation for this creative vision—yet. Only in the imagination can we fuse the separate parts and say, "Here is what I see." That's our starting point. No foundation, except first in one mind, then in several minds, then in strategy, then in action, and then and only then in the numbers of the past.

"We'll invest our advertising, promotion, and sales resources in relation to the size of opportunity you envision," I explained. "We'll get it right as we go. We'll find the right accountability of invested resources to financial outcome as we go. We'll create something new, and we'll be financially successful at it."

But you can't be imaginative and creative in business without also reflecting rationally on what you're trying to achieve. I have a vision that industrialized nations want a natural deodorant or a toothpaste that isn't a mouthful of synthetic chemicals. For me, to have such a vision is actually to see, in my mind's eye, people in a valley beyond the horizon, using natural products, trying to get closer to nature. That vision gives me a confidence that helps encourage my executives, my chemist, and all my employees to make the product come to life. But the vision is not going to happen without a lot of thought, discussion, and rational argument. Genuine creativity isn't going with whatever pops into your mind, any more than art is merely throwing paint onto a canvas. Structure is required. A *plan* of attack is necessary. And that's reason's department.

I've been thinking about the creative imagination for a long time, and I now believe that a talented business leader can draw creativity out of his executives that they themselves didn't even know was there. It requires changing your business style, opening up your company, and opening up your own mind in order to open up and honor the minds and imaginations of your employees.

I think it also requires changing the interior design of your office spaces.

THE CREATIVE CIRCLE

Creativity requires some give-and-take, dialogue, storytelling. At Tom's we found that the best way to generate creative dialogue is in "the circle."

As proud as I am about the company grants we've made to Native American groups, I'm even prouder of one of the things they gave Tom's of Maine for free—the talking circle. In many Native American cultures, the circle is the basis for ritual gatherings, representing the idea that everything is connected to everything else. (When I learned that, I couldn't help thinking about Jonathan Edwards's insights about "being is relation" and my own diagram illustrating business as a circle of interconnected circles.) I decided to adapt the talking circle to the modern business as a way to improve employees' ability to listen to one another and solve problems together. Creatively.

The circle has made it easier for us to listen to each other, no matter how diverse we, or are views, might be. The company must be an *interdependent* body. Every part—from the CEO to the production line and warehouse loading docks—can contribute to the creative process and the rational strategies; every employee can help advance the Mission and thus the business by playing his role. Or *her* role. Part of being diverse is listening to the opinions of women as well as men.

This interdependence works best, I've learned, when you hold business meetings in a circle. The circle has its own integrity. It is egalitarian in nature and effect. It suggests wholeness and completion. I find nothing more intimidating in business than a group of people sitting around a huge rectangular conference table, some of them seemingly miles away from others (usually a symbol for how far out of the power loop you actually are). Office desks, too, become a psychological as well as a physical barrier between people. I've tried to dispense with both.

For my new conference room, I had a low table made, about knee-high, where you may kneel or sit cross-legged. Anyone who prefers a chair will find one hanging on the wall, Shaker style. The table is there for papers or notes or a cup of whatever, but it will not be in anyone's way, physically or psychologically. If you come into my office, you'll find that I've arranged the space so that you won't have to sit on the other side of a big, shiny power desk. I have a desk, of course, a lovely one of cherrywood, but the decor of the room is set up so that I can move my chair over to a circle of other chairs to sit with you, not against you. It doesn't matter whether it's just you or five or six of you. We can sit in a circle. The conference rooms in the sales and marketing departments are set up in similar circle-fashion.

The circle has been introduced even into the manufacturing area of the company where we have "integrated production and quality circles." There, members of the manufacturing department can meet to talk about improving production and quality. At Tom's we view even the famous consumer mail as representative of a kind of circle:

Our packages give information and ask people to write us about their experience with the product; the contents of a letter, good and bad, will often be sent over to production or to the quality assurance department; answers are sent back to the consumer, completing the circle. Soon workers in different departments will also answer mail, linking our consumers to every department in the company.

The power of the circle is in its openness; it is the place where you are willing to "open up" and listen. And when you listen, you learn, you affirm, you support. The circle can take the idea of one person and turn it into the idea of the group. A spark of an idea is raised, discussed, argued; some disagree with it, some applaud it, others add to it, and the original idea gets better, more complex, yet more formed. One person's idea has now become everyone's idea. That brief, quiet statement from someone in your circle might turn out to be a gift of the sacred, a dynamic force.

It is still amazing to me how something as simple as a group of people talking to each other in a circle can transform the morale— and the creativity—of a company. But even more amazing to me are the results of such creativity.

THE PROFITS OF CREATIVITY

In the past few years, Tom's of Maine has experienced several extraordinary creative moments. Each time, virtually every ideal embodied in our Beliefs and Mission statements has seemed to come together in a breakthrough achievement. The creation of the deodorant outsert, for example, was the first time different departments worked together to solve a problem; it was also right in line with the Mission's commitment to the environment *and* informing our customers. The children's toothpaste, which Kate pushed through and onto the shelves, was also on target: intuitive, creative, interdepartmental, and right on the mark with the Mission. Without the Mission, we would never have come up with the information that the McCabe team needed for a brilliant strategy. Some other examples:

119

THE PART-TIME RECEPTIONIST. For years, receptionists lasted about as long as Murphy Brown's secretaries. And who could blame them? Answering the phone eight hours a day, and saying, "Hello, Tom's of Maine," is a brainless bore, as good a definition of existential hell as anyone could ever come up with. Finally, we said, no more full-time receptionists. The innovative alternative: Two full-time employees who work as secretaries also rotate daily for stints as receptionist. Incoming calls can be automatically routed to their phones. Answering the phone now is seen as "a break" from their other tasks.

The creative result: a revolving-door job gets continuity. Two employees get a break. The personnel budget saves the salary of one job position.

THE FORTY-HOUR (FOUR-DAY) WEEK. The problem: How could Tom's maintain productivity with a competent production team and not start a second shift, which would ruin the family life of those late-night workers? The ingenious solution worked out by chief financial officer Chet, who also heads up the operational side of Tom's, and the manufacturing department: ten-hour days. Actually, the line workers put in only forty hours a week, but in four days. Crews choose different four-day stints, covering the entire week, often picking up a three-day weekend.

The creative result: Manufacturing is boosted to fifty hours a week with a steady, experienced, happy crew, thus increasing overall productivity. The plan also preserved Tom's policy against working odd hours and weekends, which we all know wreaks havoc with normal family life.

Amazing stuff. So amazing for a small company that it seems almost arrogant and greedy of me to think that such extraordinary bursts of creativity ought to be the norm in our company. But the nature of our business—and the Mission—seems to assure that it will be.

A key to our creativity is encouraging people to let their imaginations rip. I try to give a new idea a chance before beating it down with reasons why it could fail. Key to our success is holding that creativity accountable. No one is allowed to do any old thing at Tom's and charge it to "creativity." Dreams and visions are one thing; outrageous fantasy and silly whims are quite another. After all, every company is accountable in the marketplace, at the bottom line.

We are, however, willing to live with mistakes. Our employees have become more imaginative and creative because they have permission to fail. But, I hasten to add, we admit to failure only after all possibilities are exhausted.

UNLOCKING CREATIVITY

Tom's is committed to competence; a high level of skill and commitment is expected of all our employees. Anyone who doesn't measure up to those expectations will have to go. Termination is never easy, but at Tom's of Maine it is always the last resort, and we always try to be fair. Sometimes the termination procedure can have amazing consequences, for the company as well as the employee.

Over the years I have discovered that a certain kind of executive will have trouble adjusting to change and to Tom's of Maine. These executives come to us with good credentials, good experience, and good intentions, but they underestimate the challenges of managing in an entrepreneurial culture. They presume that their know-how will be the muscle behind our future successes and are unwilling to learn about our culture or enter into its rhythms. Typically, they fall into a pattern in which they grow increasingly isolated and disaffected, they try to solve problems on their own, and actively or passively obstruct the workings of the team, in spite of my concerned attempts to clarify for them the job, the company, and their place in the overall scheme of things. None of these people has survived at Tom's of Maine.

But in one case, happily, things turned out differently.

One year, I realized that one of my most experienced employees was disappointing me. He had performed well for years, but Tom's was almost four times the size of the company that he had joined. The culture had changed from male to a mix of men and women. The Mission was digging down into the consciousness of more and more employees, and the challenges of the business were too complex to be solved by solo performances. I wanted everyone to open up and talk to each other, and he liked to work independently, solving his own problems. I was looking for passion and creativity; he sat in the circle, quiet and withdrawn, too willing to go along with the ideas of others. I was trying to persuade my MBAs to recognize that though we were growing exponentially in sales and profits, I didn't want the company to lose its small-town feel. As I discussed the long-range pictures with management, one-on-one, everyone seemed positively on fire with what we were doing and with understanding the challenge Tom's had set to do well by doing good—everyone except this one particular person.

After my one-on-one meeting with him, I questioned whether he belonged here. Was he still suited for this role? He was certainly not in tune with the Mission principle "to foster teamwork." I gave him another chance to prove me wrong (because I wanted to be proved wrong), and I was disappointed again. While he seemed eager enough to respond to my suggestions and ideas for his work, he didn't seem to have any ideas of his own. Were we about to lose another person who fit the problem pattern? The implications were scary.

But before I reached a final decision, I wanted to discuss this matter with some of my advisers. I confided my feelings about this employee. I welcomed disagreement, but there was none. I asked them to challenge my thinking, but they, too, were at a loss. Still open to a different perspective, I decided to discuss it with six other members of the board who might have an opinion. They, too, agreed, and admitted they had seen it coming. Lamenting the possibility of losing the big investment made in this employee over several years, they emphasized their support of my judgment.

But there was one more board member I wanted to talk to who had been unavailable. When I finally reached her, she said she would support my decision but added, "It's too bad because I know he's got the passion and creativity you're looking for. He just seems to have a block." She thought that with some professional help—the right "interpersonal training" lab, for instance—he might be able to unlock the creativity and enthusiasm for his job that she sensed was in him. I told her we had nothing to lose by postponing the decision and seeing whether he could work things out for himself and the company. That night I discussed it with Kate. "She's right," she said. "Who are we to judge that miracles can't happen to him? Miracles have happened in our own life." I relayed my decision back to my advisers and they seemed relieved. They conceded that they had realized that losing this person would have a big effect on the morale of the company. They, too, were eager to give him one more chance. It was time for a heart-to-heart talk.

I let him have it straight on: how the business was changing, his role was changing, how he needed to change; how I needed him to help identify the challenges we faced; and how we needed him to be part of the solution. We needed his ideas, his passions, his actions. I wrote him a letter, "a wake-up call," as I candidly put it.

I laid out in detail what I thought the new focus of his job should be. The emphasis was on creativity. He simply had to go beyond the basics of his job description and bring his passion and spirit into the job and his relationships. As I drafted this very difficult letter, I began to noodle around with some ideas I had about how he might increase his chances for meeting our expectations for him, which were nothing less than a kind of personal and professional self-transformation.

I began the letter thinking I was doing this person a big favor. By the time I finished, I realized he had done *me* a big favor. As I drafted it, I had come up with a new idea that might not only help him but help me and the rest of my executives unleash our own creativity. I began to see the "creative manager" as one person made up of several selves—five to be exact. I recommended these different selves to him. Here are some excerpts from that letter:

1. THE CREATIVE SELF: The creative in any of us springs from a sense of freedom and a need to connect or express ourself interconnectedly.

He needed to find ways to unlock his creative self and bring his passion to his new challenges. So do we all. He didn't think he was a very creative person. But our board specialist saw signs of creativity in him. All of us are likely to be more creative than we (or others) suspect. The challenge is to let our creativity loose, to give ourselves a chance to be creative. At Tom's we've tried to increase the odds for creativity—by encouraging openness, by the circle, by breaking down the false barriers of hierarchy and departmental infighting, by living the Mission.

2. THE AMBITIOUS SELF: Channel your competitive energy toward your work. Be unashamed of your enthusiasm for your products and for your company, and your commitment to make a difference, in your own way, in the world.

3. THE INTERDEPENDENT SELF: There is no independence at Tom's of Maine. You are necessarily *linked* with both a hierarchy (in which you have a boss and people working for you) and a circle of teammates (in which you participate in the overall motion and flow of the business energy and strategy). Think about how you can *contribute* to the flow in both the hierarchy and the circle. *Collaborate* with your teammates, interdepartmentally. *Connect* where you can with businesses outside the company.

4. THE RATIONAL SELF: *Organize* your people, financial resources, and time toward clear objectives. *Interpret* the data you experience.

5. THE NO SELF: Let go of your ego. Discover how you fit into a larger sphere of activity in which others are being themselves and contributing to their worth.

I had never written a perspective on performance like it. (I have never seen one like it.) But once I had finished the letter, I realized that it was a pretty good guide for increasing the odds on creativity from any manager locked into a day-to-day framework of analysis. I decided to use this model for all my managers.

Above all, I learned that even something as unpleasant as figuring out how to fire someone can turn into a creative process, for all concerned. Throughout the process I remained open. I preferred not to have to let this person go. I didn't pretend to know all the answers. I sought counsel, which came to his rescue—and mine—with one of those sacred gifts of intuition. She saw something that I didn't, that *he* didn't. Her insight became the key I needed to make my decision; when I sat down to write the memo it was her gift that inspired me to come up with the insight of the five selves. Here was my partnership with the divine at work! I had stayed open, flexible, and asked for help, and because I did, I came up with another gift, a new way of "being in relation" and helping people to see how they are in relation to others. It is a new management tool that helps us all define identity at Tom's. It is now up to that employee to prove that he is worthy of such a gift. (He has thanked me and said, "I'm ready to start anew.")

In fact, he did. We both started over, creating a new relationship. He appreciated my honesty. He recognized that we were both speaking from the heart; there were no hidden agendas. I had criticized his work, but I had also offered positive suggestions on how he might change. "It's easy to focus on the negative," he told me later. "But unless we begin to look at the good in the individual, we'll destroy the positive of the whole."

In retrospect, I'm not only happy I searched for the good in this individual, I'm relieved. At this stage of the company's evolution, I need his experience more than ever. We've looked back on that tense time together, talked about it, and now see it in its complexity. I can view the situation better from his perspective: His job may have turned a bit dull. I may have been expecting too much. But the job is not dull now, and he seems to have risen to the challenge. Better still, he and I have now begun working together closely and effectively. Encouraged to be himself, he has let his passions loose, gotten excited about the business again, and is doing terrific things.

The message of this particular experience at Tom's: Let the

intuitive guide us all. Creative solutions will follow. Imagination is too sacred to lose. Nurture and respect it. Turbo-charged powerboats and fixed agendas and methods of being keep us from the "feel" of our business. Sail into open waters, and navigate along with the winds and the tides. Allow yourself to get in touch with the insights and creativity—the sacred—around you, and let it guide you. The reason big companies buy small companies is that the giants lose their capacity to be creative and innovative. They are too burdened by rationality and analysis. Let your imagination fly. Trust your intuition. Create opportunities for your managers to be creative. You're already great at crunching numbers. By combining rationality and creativity, you can help your company become great.

MANAGING CREATIVITY

Intuition and creativity in business are interlinked, but unless you exercise these attributes, you won't become skillful in using them. Through experience, you become able to distinguish between intuitive ideas that simply *must* be implemented and those that need further refinement.

- Encourage people to dream. Ask them to put aside the historical view of the company and imagine its most successful future. Don't censor their visions, no matter how farfetched. Out of their individual visions you will claim more creativity for the company.

- Creative responses and solutions to problems often come out of situations that seem unresolvable. Think of some classic disagreements you have had out of which a satisfactory resolution was forged—not just a resolution you preferred, but one that truly worked at all levels and made your business or product or team work better than ever before. Identify the opposing view-points, and how the fusion of this decision or solution was effected.

- Tap the power of the circle. Hold meetings where the seating arrangement values participants equally. Remove desks and other physical barriers between people, even in one-on-one meetings.

- Reflect on the decision-making teams with which you work most frequently. What is the dynamic process that characteristically takes place? Are there people whose interjections and different ideas you regularly discount? Do these people actually act as quiet catalysts to creative solutions? Who are the people whose intuitions and creative ideas you trust? What is it about their presentation that persuades you? Why do you "go" with their arguments? Are there regular dissenters or gadflies who contribute to or hamper the process? How could you manage differently the give-and-take of these problem-solving sessions to optimize the process?

- Rethink your performance review system. In addition to setting goals and tasks to be accomplished, let it help you get at the five business selves. Ask your employees what they need from you to express their creative self more fully.

INTENTIONAL
DIVERSITY: CREATING
COMPLEX BEAUTY

N ot long ago, Tom's of Maine needed a salesperson in southern
California. We did what any company does when it has to hire
someone three thousand miles away: We went to a professional
recruiting firm, described the job, and asked them to come up with a
short list of qualified candidates for us to interview. There was one
other requirement: We wanted a diverse pool of candidates, especially women. Two months later, the recruiter returned with a list of
three candidates—all white men.

I was furious. I explained to our vice-president of sales and the
recruiter that filling this job gave us an opportunity to add some

diversity to our ranks. I also leveled with the recruiter: "We simply aren't going to interview your three white men because you didn't hear us. We said, 'Bring some women among those finalists.' " After all, the recruiter was choosing from one of the most diverse regions of America, filled with talented African-Americans, Hispanics, and Asians. The recruiting firm was amazed because typically its clients would say, "Make this an equal opportunity position," and the headhunter would respond, "What do you really want?" Thus, everyone manages to sidestep the equal opportunity laws. I made it clear to the recruiting firm that we weren't playing that game.

A few weeks later, the recruiter returned with another list of three candidates—two of them women, both highly qualified. We hired one, and she quickly became one of our top salespeople.

Tom's of Maine is an equal opportunity employer *not* simply because it's the law, but because it's good for our company. We have learned to see that hiring and having *differences* within the company—not just in the color of people's skin or in their accents, but in their education, their experience, their background, and their abilities—is a business advantage, a *major* business advantage, besides being a moral responsibility. *Learning* is the operative word for me and the company. For while Tom's of Maine is totally committed to diversity, this commitment didn't just happen. It wasn't easy to persuade everyone at Tom's that we could all profit from diversity, personally as well as financially. It's human nature to love the self, to be comfortable with people like you and uneasy among "foreigners"; it's quite natural to say, "My clan is number one."

Today, however, we live in an increasingly pluralistic society. America will soon be more brown than white. (Los Angeles, the nation's second-largest city, is already nearly 40 percent Hispanic.) All these different people from different cultural traditions and with different religious beliefs are bound to have different values, some of which are likely to be incompatible. No one in our society, especially not those of us in business who serve and profit from these diverse people—all potential customers—can run the risk of thinking our way is the best way. Our values must be accountable to a larger society. To find our way to that bigger group, we have to include more of its members—women, people of color, the disadvantaged, and others from different backgrounds and life experiences unfamiliar to us.

"Keep it simple, stupid," is a slogan much admired in American business. Bunk! In my opinion and experience, keeping it simple may be only the first sign of how much we're missing. I ought to know; it was a kind of complacency I myself once embraced. But I've now come to believe that diversity is not just an obligation. At Tom's of Maine, we have discovered to our delight that diversity is a value that you can translate into a competitive advantage. It is the difference between limiting yourself to a single cultural view and achieving a fullness and wholeness by welcoming differences. It is about creating goodness.

So let me tell you how I discovered the beauty of diversity. My company is hardly where I want it to be on this count, but we're working on it. For anyone who wants to follow us, I think I can save you some hardship.

HOW I CHANGED
FROM A YOUNG FOGEY

Six or so years ago, Tom's of Maine was your basic male-dominated company, with men heading every department. I didn't even give it much thought. After all, my board was more than one-third women and Kate was deeply involved in the company and instrumental in its early successes. I considered myself an executive who was comfortable with women and respectful of what they could bring to a business. After all, my own wife had helped me found a company. And how could a man with two talented daughters not be sensitive to the dreams and ambitions of women?

But at divinity school, in a class about "Miracles in the Gospels" taught by the feminist theologian Elisabeth Schüssler-Fiorenza, we were working our way through the Gospel According to Mark, with particular emphasis on the relation between Jesus and his disciples during Christ's final days. The author of Mark makes it very clear that from the time between Jesus's arrest and his disappearance from the tomb, his most loyal "disciples" were the women who followed him, not the men. On his way to Jerusalem, before his arrest, when an onlooker criticizes a woman who is anointing him for wasting valuable oil, an angry Jesus replies, "Let her alone. She has done a beautiful thing. . . . And truly I say to you, wherever the gospel is preached in the world, what she has done will be told in memory of her." Judas betrayed Jesus; Peter, "the rock" on which Christ said he would build his church, deserted him; and as he died on the cross, his male disciples were nowhere in sight. But his women followers were at the cross; they also appeared at the tomb.

During these classes I became increasingly aware, to my horror, that I had not given my wife all the credit she deserved. From the time we started the company, I had felt that I played a more important role in those business decisions than Kate. As the class continued, I began to value Kate's contribution to Tom's of Maine more and more, and I felt ashamed of my own arrogance. Finally, I admitted my shame to my classmates, and afterward some of the women thanked me for being so honest about my male prejudices. It helped, but from then on I resolved to give Kate more credit for her supporting role to me and for her own individual contribution to R&D and her sensitivity to people in the workplace.

At age forty-four, co-founder and CEO of a successful company, I was finally beginning to learn something about the value of diversity. Intellectually, I had been opposed to prejudice and racism since childhood. My parents taught me to despise ethnic slurs and anti-Semitism. My father told me that in doing business with Jews, he admired their respect for the family, which he too saw as sacred, and that became the common ground between him and his Jewish business relations. At a Quaker prep school in New England, equality was drilled into us. But once I had a growing business and decided that I wanted it to grow more, I believed that I had to turn to traditional business practices, to learn from the powerful majority how to become more "professional."

At Harvard, however, I soon learned that if I really wanted

wisdom, I'd better listen to the powerless. I began to learn something about humility. It's not an easy virtue to learn when you've been to all-male schools and worked in large corporations, as I had, or if you've been to business school and earned big incomes, in the case of many of my own top executives. But at Harvard I sat in class and hung out with women, young men, Asians, Indians, Europeans, and homosexuals. I became friends with all sorts of people. I spent my time in class and outside discussing very important philosophical and theological issues, as well as ordinary stuff, with people who were *different* from me. Very different. (As different as they might have appeared to me, imagine how a fortysomething refugee from an American corporation looked to those divinity students!)

I began to sense the beauty of it all—and Jonathan Edwards, once again, explained why. Unconcerned with the political and social justice of equal opportunity, Edwards conveyed the richness, firmness, and solidarity of what he called "complex beauty."

DIVERSITY AS COMPLEX BEAUTY

"Particular disproportions greatly add to general beauty," Edwards wrote in his essay "The Mind." According to Edwards, the more complex the beauty, the more apparent its disproportions, the more intense that beauty becomes, the greater its excellency. Edwards realized that such apparent "disproportions," when viewed from higher ground, turn into "complex beauties."

That made perfect *business* sense to me. Up close, all those different skin colors, religious beliefs, cultural traditions, and genders mixed in one place can look pretty chaotic. But you had to see those customers from different perspectives, you had to listen to different points of view. Surely, if I wanted to sell natural toothpaste or deodorant to a diverse population, I would have to have feedback from a diversity of sources. If I wanted to serve my customers and treat them respectfully, then I'd better know something about them.

Like every other company, my managers and I had been inclined to hire in our own image. We were looking for a kind of sameness, the comfort of the familiar. What we had forgotten was that pure, unadulterated iron is not strong enough to build bridges. Only when it is combined with other alloys—with different metals, "impurities"—does iron become steel. Sameness, like a dozen red roses, does have its beauty. But complex beauty, Edwards teaches, is more intense. The greater the complexity, the greater the excellency, according to Edwards. The effort to resolve complex differences, recognizing their not-so-obvious relations, standing back and seeing how it all fits together like wild flowers in a field, is to watch apparent discord turn into something that is not only genuinely beautiful but a model of excellency. Colleen Myers, as I mentioned, has a law degree and a master's in divinity. What might have struck a more traditional company as an odd combination of credentials turned out to be a perfect fit for Tom's of Maine.

DIVERSITY AS A GIFT

Like most businessmen—and here I emphasize the *men* part of that word—I believed that authority and power are synonymous. I often wielded my power to prove my authority, and my employees quaked in their boots, appropriately intimidated. In divinity school I began to recognize that my power to intimidate my employees was likely to intimidate their creativity. If you're constantly second-guessing the boss to keep your job, you're not about to take any chances. And no company will succeed without someone taking risks.

Then I reread Saint Paul's Letter to the Corinthians and was struck by what he said in Chapter 12 about the various gifts different people have. "There are varieties of gifts," Paul pointed out, "but the same Spirit." I began to see how we could be different individuals but part of the same common spirit, or company; our "varieties of gifts" could be assembled in some profitable way. Later in the same chapter, Paul compared the Christian community to a "body"—"Just as the body is one and has many members, and all the members of the body, though many, are one. . . . For the body does not consist of one member but of many." Though different, one body part is as valuable as the other, and all the parts have to function *interdependently* to make up a complete body.

Just like a successful company—one company, comprising many different parts, and gifts.

DIVERSITY AS INTERDEPENDENCE

Saint Paul's suggestion that the whole depends on each part has been confirmed and enriched for me by a recent book that has nothing to do with religion or theology, at least on the face of it—*The Diversity of Life,* by Harvard zoologist Edward O. Wilson. Wilson explores the diversity of the rain forest, showing how every creature, every event, no matter how tiny, is interconnected in amazing ways.

Biological diversity is the key to the maintenance of the world as we know it. . . . It is diversity by which life builds and saturates the rain forest. And diversity has carried life beyond, to the harshest environments on earth. . . . [It is] the property that makes resilience possible.

I began seeing diversity in a company as a kind of ecosystem—a swirling, living mass of variety and difference, but all working together in a creative, vital way. Customers, different in their own ways and backgrounds, also contribute to this diversity. It was not long before I realized that the more sensitive my executives and I could become to the differences of the people we were trying to serve, and the more perspectives we could plug into our discussions about product design, business strategy, and customer service, the more broadly the company could range to meet its financial objectives. We had to listen to as many different sources as possible, both inside and outside the company.

With all this evidence, I set out to make my company and its practices as diverse as possible.

BRINGING MORE WOMEN
INTO MANAGEMENT

From divinity school I sent a letter to the board and my management team. "We have got to bring more women to the company, particularly in management," I wrote. The board, with four women out of eleven members, was behind me. Once the recruiters understood that our commitment to hiring women was for real, the numbers shot up as quickly as the company grew. Now Tom's is 40 percent female; two departments are headed by women; and the crucial marketing department has fourteen women and two men.

It was not an easy transition for the men of Tom's of Maine to make, myself included. The fact is that when you've grown up in a culture where males are favored for leadership positions and power, it's just plain odd all of a sudden to have women sitting at the same table offering their opinions or, more shocking to most men, disagreeing with you. I felt the strangeness of it, and so did my executives. It reminded me of attending class on Saturday morning at my all-male college with weekend dates present. On those occasions at Trinity, a few young women, engaged by the topic at hand, would dominate the discussion, *our* discussion, and I would sit there wondering, "Who the hell do they think they are?"

Fortunately, our company had Kate as our first woman executive model, the icebreaker. She was not just my wife but a co-founder and equal partner as well as vice-president of R&D, thus an executive who had much to contribute to business strategy. After another woman became head of marketing, we hired a woman to head up community life. The presence of three women executives began to affect our business planning.

The women have a different take on things, a new perspective that has quickly enhanced our company objectives. As a company whose very identity is its relationship to its loyal and well-informed customers, we have to be very intentional about respecting those customers, providing them with as much information as possible and being available to them when they write or phone. The women in

135

marketing seem to have a better feel for customers, probably because traditionally in our culture women have been more responsible for shopping than men and are more experienced consumers. Caring about the facts of a product themselves, the women executives at Tom's want to know how our products are made, why certain ingredients are chosen over others, and what the particular advantages are, and they seem more willing to deliver the facts to our customers.

As a result, Tom's has become more attentive and responsive to the needs of our customers. The copy written about the products and the company Mission for packages and inserts is more informative. The attention to consumer mail has increased. Phone interaction with our customers, who are constantly calling us at our Kennebunk offices, has increased; our customer relations people often spend as much as twenty minutes with each caller.

This time-intensive involvement with our customers strengthens our relations; they see that we're not dismissing them as objects or putting them into "categories of respondents" A, B, C, D, or E—the standard business approach. The usual company policy is, "Give them no more than three minutes on the phone and send them a form letter." But we want to know what our customers think; their responses help us become more aware of the diversity of our customer base. The information we get from them we feed back into our marketing strategies. Their suggestions help us improve our products. Diversity does tend to slow you down in one sense, but at Tom's of Maine we recognize that slow gear can be a good thing; it allows you to discuss a problem more, it requires you to listen more intently to different perspectives. In another sense, by making as sure as possible that the outcome will be strong and good, it saves you time and trouble down the line.

Tom's of Maine is about listening, and the fourteen women (and two men) we have in our marketing department today make us better listeners.

Do I think that women are better than men at dealing with customers? Without debating the merits or demerits of the feminist struggle in America over the past twenty years, let me simply say that I don't think that men are incapable of being more sensitive or responsive to other people. The two men in our marketing department are cases in point: tireless and responsive to community groups eager for our sponsorship, they show their care and compassion for the homeless, the needy, and AIDS victims. Nonetheless, it's beyond debate that women in our culture traditionally have been the listeners, the supporters, the nurturers, the servers. This has given them a different point of view. African-Americans, Hispanics, Native Americans, and other "minority groups" can also see the world quite differently from powerful white males. A business that seeks out the opinions of diverse peoples is not just showing good business sense and respect for others; in our increasingly diverse market it is plain good business practice.

Each of us is inclined to think that what we see of the world is all there is to see. But Alfred North Whitehead reminds us that the different lives we lead, the paths we've walked down, influence what we see amid the chaos of a given moment. If you don't believe this, assemble a circle of eight people from your company from different walks of life and ask them to discuss a specific business problem. You are likely to get at least eight different perspectives—profit, customer relations, environmental concerns, effect on morale in the workplace, personnel problems, questions of fairness, the board's point of view, shareholder concerns. What one business leader can keep all these points of view in his head at once?

By opening up our eyes, diversity can make us more visionary managers. My hope is that the presence of so many women managers at Tom's of Maine will inspire their male colleagues to look at issues and problems from different angles. The differences between us contribute to a special kind of wholeness or completeness. Therefore, we need to bring our differences into the circle, into the team, so that we can all become better at understanding how much both sexes are capable of. If that happens, soon women will be able to assert their views, opinions, and commitment to certain outcomes without worrying about being branded as "too pushy" or "aggressive."

Over and over again at Tom's we have seen how diversity leads the way to a better, more productive, more *human* work life. And the benefits from diversity are hardly limited to hiring women executives. Consider what we all learn from June, a person with special needs who cleans our offices and who asked me for an office.

137

June, fifty-one, has never been afraid to speak her mind. If she's dissatisfied with a brand of floor cleaner or a change in her day's regime, she lets me know, up close and personal. One day, she found sixty dollars in cash in my wastebasket. "You're stupid," she told me in no uncertain terms, then proceeded to make her opinion clear to everyone else in the company.

Sometimes someone needs to tell the boss he's stupid, but no one except June dares. She's different. When June likes you, she hugs you. (I'm pleased to say she hugs me all the time, so I must be doing something right.) When she's unhappy, she speaks her mind. Part of a program Tom's of Maine established with the Community Support Services, which works with developmentally and physically disadvantaged adults, June proves every day that among the complex organizational charts and strategies and the unavoidable stress of business, there's a place for feelings. If you were to walk into our offices and see June, you might think her out of place. Slow and deliberate in her work, she completes a task, then checks it off on her clipboard, where her instructions are described graphically (a picture of a wastebasket, a broom, a mop, windows). But June's special developmental needs, her apparent "disproportion," to use Jonathan Edwards's word, ultimately makes a lot of sense at Tom's of Maine. Different as she might be, June fits in. By showing us how easy it is to stop and say "How are you today?" she shows how easy it is to care about our fellow workers. By her capacity to love and even hug her fellow employees (including the CEO), she has added intensity and beauty to the company.

THE PERSONAL
CHALLENGES OF DIVERSITY

The "varieties of gifts" that people bring to work are not always so obvious to the company, or even to the employees themselves. The policy at Tom's of Maine that employees should try to give five percent of their *work time* to some kind of community service or volunteer project has opened many employees up to the possibilities of life.

Paula, a middle manager at Tom's, volunteered to help out in a community project called Very Special Arts, which helps expose handicapped children to the visual and tactile arts. The job required a lot of attention to tasks and details, which appealed to Paula. She got involved; "Before I knew it," she told me, "the director of the program asked me to coordinate a daylong event involving six hundred children and teachers from the area." She got many others from the company involved, and Paula's volunteer work became an exciting part of her life, as well as a revelation about her own talents. When Paula told me about this work, I asked her whether it had taught her anything about herself. She grinned, sat back, and said, "Well, yes it has. I've been living in my little box, and this got me to come out, and now I'm directing the whole thing."

Paula's ability to run a big project had come as news to her; it was certainly not a skill of which her bosses at Tom's of Maine were aware. I asked her to write a memo to her superiors about what she was doing with Very Special Arts, and she did. Here was a case where a woman simply volunteered some time, went to where the needy people were, asked "What can I do for you?"—and her life got changed. Paula learned that when you go to where the needy are, you had better be prepared for your life to change. Now she comes to work and does her job, which she likes; but her real passion is her volunteer work. I have a feeling the company will figure out a way to take advantage of Paula's newfound talents and passion.

Renn, our production supervisor, also tried a new challenge, and it sent him in a direction that he would never have imagined. When a local high school asked Renn if he had a job on the production line for a Down's syndrome boy named Nate, Renn brought him in, got to know him a bit, and decided he could do the job. Renn was eager to do his part, but he later told me that though he knew it was, as he put it, "my human responsibility to treat people with respect no matter who they are," he had welcomed the opportunity to put his beliefs to the test. The challenge was to make Nate a responsible contributor to the best of his ability on the toothpaste production line. Nate's fellow workers pitched in, teaching him the various tasks along the line, putting toothpaste into tubes, cartoning the tubes, and loading the pallets.

But there were problems. Sometimes Nate would show up at work, walk over into the corner, sit down, and refuse to work. Renn felt he had to convince Nate that sitdown strikes are unacceptable behavior for a working man, that when you work on the production line, you've got to pull your own weight. But how? He tried telling this to Nate straightforwardly, with no effect. He left him alone to stew. No change. Mystified but still challenged, Renn decided to enroll in a fifteen-week special course at a nearby college to learn more about people like Nate. What he quickly found out was that you have to treat Down's syndrome people as equals, with respect and responsibility. They do not want special favors or special accommodations.

Renn brought that sense of equality back to his relationship with Nate, who has become a reliable worker on the line and performs virtually as well as anyone else, station by station. Nate's now a happy, responsible young man who definitely earns his paycheck. "Just as machines require attention with cleaning and oiling on a regular basis, I learned that people are no different," Renn explains. "They require care, they need to be attended to, they need to be treated with respect. Nate has helped me become that sensitive to the needs of people." Renn decided to sign up for another fifteen-week course, this time in sociology. "I want to get a view of humanity beyond the production area, how to deal with the 'mixed tribe,'" he explains. The company is paying for Renn to take his fifteen-week sociology course.

Paula and Renn are great examples of how diversity can sneak up on you—and change your life. But making diversity part of the essence of any company is a major change in itself, and despite its proven benefits, many employees would prefer to see big changes happen to someone else's company.

THE CHALLENGE TO DIVERSITY

Even at Tom's of Maine where I, the co-founder and CEO, was eager to have a more diverse company, we decided, four years after I sent the word that the company had to hire more women, that the company wasn't working hard enough toward this goal of diversity. The board had already amended the Mission and Beliefs statements with a commitment to "competence." Now it wanted to put our commitment to diversity in writing. Echoing Saint Paul, we drafted this for the Beliefs Statement:

 We believe that people bring different gifts and perspectives to the team and that a strong team is founded on a variety of gifts.

To the Mission Statement, the board added the goal:

 To honor and seek a diversity of gifts and perspectives in our work together.

When we brought these amendments to the company at large, the employees bought the Beliefs Statement on diversity but balked at the Mission version. *Seek* was a red flag. The implied initiative to *look* far and wide for new talents bothered them. "Why can't you honor and encourage the gifts that are here rather than think you have to go *outside* the company to find them?" someone asked. The resentment was wide and strong.

They had a point. After all, according to the Statement of Beliefs, employees at Tom's are supposed to believe "that human beings and nature are worthy of our respect." Wasn't the board's eagerness to go outside the company to fill jobs evidence of its lack of recognition of the abilities of its current employees? The board, however, defended its more explicit commitment to diversity by pointing out that *because* of our commitment to respecting human beings, we had to nurture diversity. In an effort to encourage creativity and high performance, Tom's was trying to get away from the traditional business practices of treating employees as interchangeable "tools" (or as Kant might put it, as "means" rather than "ends in themselves"—worthy for what they are and not for their utility). It followed that if the kind of high performance we were after could be better found in an employee not yet working at Tom's, then we wanted to hire her.

Equal opportunity efforts, whether pure window dressing or a genuine desire for diversity, have provoked a backlash across the country. White males especially feel that they're being displaced and, worse, sometimes by job candidates who are not as experienced or well trained as they. Cries of reverse discrimination have been heard by businesspeople and executives around the country as well as in the federal courts (which are no less confused as to what to do about the issue).

We listened to our employees, talked through their resentment, and this is what we heard: The company was not doing enough to affirm the "gifts" that it already had. Top management had to work harder to reach out to learn more about the skills of its existing employees and explore ways for people to contribute more to the team. The board, however, refused to yield on its determination to find the best employees possible, even if it required going outside the company. While understanding fears of the unknown and of outsiders and the defensiveness among the employees, the company could not veer from its ambition to be the very best at what it did, even if that meant looking for talent outside the company or outside of Maine. It was the only time since the Mission was initiated that the Tom's of Maine board had used its authority. But the board did agree to rewrite the new statement on diversity for the Mission, to accommodate the justifiable concern among employees that they might be overlooked. The Mission now reads:

 To recognize, encourage, and seek a diversity of gifts and perspectives in our work life.

The company has already begun efforts to take advantage of the obvious gifts of current employees and to try to flush out the latent skills of others. Professional growth is now a top priority at Tom's; we've surveyed employees and management about the kinds of training and courses they want. The community life department has already begun publishing a list of programs and courses within a fifty-mile radius of Kennebunk. In-house, we've begun working with our management to help them become better leaders, particularly with an eye to the guiding principles of the Mission.

When a job opens up at Tom's of Maine, our employees are

encouraged to apply. But they are also aware that no job will be filled until the opening is advertised in the local press as well as in newspapers outside Maine and all the best candidates have been interviewed. For every job, it is open season. The only advantage our employees have is that, if the choice is between two finalists equally qualified for a job and one is a Tom's of Maine employee, the Tom's person will get the job. Otherwise, hiring from within is bound only to increase the homogeneity of any company. This also holds for new management positions that open up—no executive working for the company has an automatic lock on the job. They have to apply like anyone else. I don't leave the executive search outside the company entirely in the hands of a recruiter either; these jobs are also posted at Tom's of Maine. To reach outside may not be the kindest or friendliest practice, but it is the one that best serves our goals of diversity and competence.

Tom's of Maine does not seek to hire women or ethnics or people of color because that is the law, or even because it is fashionable or "politically correct." We are seeking diversity because it is good for the company, *profitable* for the company. Diversity heightens the value of interdependence in the company. The more we talk to each other, the better our ideas and solutions are. The more different our own people are, the broader our perspective will be. The more differences we are put in touch with, the more progress we will make as people, managers, and company.

RECOGNIZING DIVERSITY

Last fall, the board, shareholders, and staff of Tom's of Maine met together in an old barn on the coast. We ended the day in a circle on a sun-drenched hillside. To the east was the Atlantic Ocean; to the west what Native Americans call Turtle Island—and what we call North America. It seemed an ideal spot for a workshop on diversity. Father Philip Allen, the newest member of the Tom's of Maine board, spoke movingly of the pain of dislocation that Native Americans have felt since the arrival of Europeans on the continent; but he also spoke with pride and hope of the great strides his people are making to conserve their heritage and communities. The other speaker was Dana Mitchell, a member of the Penobscots, a people who were living in what is now Maine when the Europeans arrived. Dana, a friend of mine and a member of the elder's circle of the American Indian Council, expressed his own anger about the loss of tribal lands and discrimination against Native Americans. He talked about his efforts to help young Native Americans feel pride in their backgrounds and traditional ways that have persisted in the face of centuries of domination.

I sensed that day that Father Allen and Dana had found one of their most open and vulnerable audiences in the people from Tom's of Maine. All day we had been discussing diversity, and I had the feeling that what the people in the audience had learned about each other—and themselves—made Dana's and Father Allen's stories seem a lot less alien or different than they might have seemed even a day before. That morning, Asherah Cinnamon, from the National Coalition Building Institute, a recognized leader in teaching team-building and conflict mediation, led us through "Ups/Downs," an exercise designed to help people experience pride in who they are and where they come from. She explained that only when we are comfortable with the core of our identity—our race, sex, religion, social class, education, and so on—can we be comfortable embracing people different from us.

"All those who were born poor, please stand up!" Ashera asked. People rose—and not always the people one had assumed started out poor. "All those raised Catholic . . . Jewish . . . who never graduated from high school . . . who wanted children but didn't have them." I was amazed. Though I knew of cases of infertility among married women, I hadn't considered the single women who longed for a child. It was very moving. The categories continued, and the Tom's people stood up and sat down. Preconceptions, prejudices, and stereotypes rose and fell too. Tom's of Maine is still basically a white company, but I was impressed by the diversity of backgrounds and experiences, some joyful, some embarrassing, that were revealed during that simple exercise. Unexpected connections were made, and similarities discovered. "I didn't know you grew up poor!" said one employee to an executive. "I didn't know you couldn't have a baby," said one woman to another. "I didn't know you were Catholic." And so it went, one revelation after another.

Afterward, Colleen, who had helped organize the event, made her own revelation to me: "I came into the circle in that barn that morning with a tingling spine and nervous stomach," she said. She was aware of the risk that "Ups/Downs" would only encourage people's tendency to stereotype others. Would it give people more reason to dislike their fellow workers, more ammunition for teasing each other? Such questions hung in her mind as Asherah began the exercise. "It was with a rush of relief and affection for the community of Tom's of Maine that I watched one person after another rise and claim their identity in the presence of all—the points of pride as well as the secret shames and the hidden wounds of racism, sexism, and all the other isms with which we surround and isolate ourselves."

All it took was one game, one *profound* game, and suddenly the people of Tom's of Maine had become more understanding. They recognized that they, too, were surrounded by differences—differences they had never even perceived—and the differences were they. The people of Tom's of Maine had discovered the goodness of diversity.

Diversity is not only a kind of understanding; nor is it just a mosaic of employees who have walked different paths. Diversity is also a value that creates excellence. It ought to be at the heart of your entire business strategy.

MANAGING BY DIVERSITY

Within the past year, an important sales administration position opened up. There were two finalists. One was a man with considerable consumer-brand sales and marketing experience, a very strong candidate. The other was a woman with an extensive retail and merchandising background who had worked for another company that cared about values, particularly respect for other people. Both had done their homework and were well briefed on what they thought I cared about most. In describing his management style, the man discussed "facilitating" this and "facilitating" that.

I pressed him on what he meant by "facilitate." He responded with a story about a sales concept he had created for a product line. "I facilitated it very well," he said. "I presented it to sales, presented it to marketing, and my concept came out at the end of the process just the way it went in, with no changes." Just as I had expected, this man had no idea of facilitated leadership.

The way we understand it at Tom's is to listen, to reflect, to share our own response, and to be committed to an improved outcome. It is definitely not about powering something through without a scratch on it. Our view is that no matter how good an idea is, it can be made better by the contribution of the people in the group. We presuppose that the variety of the perspectives will intensify the goodness and beauty of an idea. He didn't seem to get that.

By contrast, the woman candidate, who never even mentioned the buzzword *facilitate,* seemed to be a natural at connecting and drawing forth the ideas of others. She understood the integrity of ethical process—listen, reflect, share, affirm. She could stand in the shoes of the buyer and the merchandiser because she'd been both. She could be the link that brought sales and marketing together when the heads of the two departments were having trouble accomplishing that. She was open, articulate, and energetic. Though she didn't realize it at the time, she was proving to me that she had the experience and the personality to be a natural facilitator of other people's gifts.

She had the qualities to fit into our company because she already seemed to understand, intuitively, the power of the circle.

THE CIRCLE AND THE TRIANGLE

At Tom's of Maine, two different paradigms guide our business style. As I discussed in chapter 6, the circle is how we gather together to listen to a problem, to share and listen to opinions, and to function as a team in generating a new creative solution. The circle is not a place where anyone's personal agenda is ramrodded through. Your individual responsibility as a member of the circle is to listen to the others, reflect, then assert your own point of view. You facilitate by encouraging another person to say more about their idea; it's a conversation of people who believe that the outcome will be co-created.

We also have the triangle, which symbolizes the structure of authority at Tom's, differentiated by the value of a particular job. A vice-president has a different job value from a product manager. This kind of hierarchy has nothing to do with power or creativity; it's simply how decisions get made. In the course of every decision, there is someone at the top of that triangle, an authority on that team.

The circle is there for listening and openness, for dialogue and co-creating; the triangle is there for the structure, to remind every-body of who gets to make the decision, at every level of the company. Everyone at Tom's of Maine is accountable to someone else. We listen to everyone, but consensus does not reign. Someone has the authority in every circle but is accountable to another with more authority. A worker on the production line is accountable to his supervisor, who is accountable to the manufacturing manager, who is accountable to the executive vice-president, who is accountable to the president, who is accountable to the board, who are accountable to the owners, who are accountable to the common good.

And so these two systems, the circle and the triangle, come together into a different paradigm of doing business, affirming the contribution that everyone makes to the process but within the tradition of authority. Everyone is equal in the circle, but someone in the triangle is in charge.

Management Organization

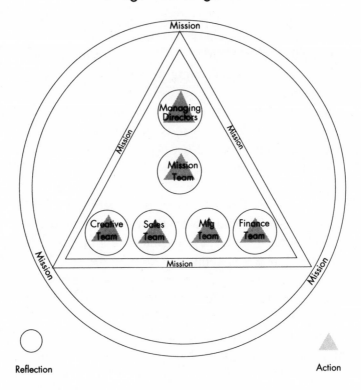

Reflection   Action

DIVERSITY AS
TOTAL BUSINESS STRATEGY

Diversity is not just an ideal for the workplace; it is also a marketing strategy. We market some twenty-three different products all under the Tom's of Maine name. (This contrasts with Procter & Gamble, which markets its toothpaste under the name Crest and its deodorant as Sure.) We believe in a diversity of products supporting

148

one common brand—Tom's of Maine—and we believe this makes Tom's increasingly excellent as a company. We also have chosen to remain a regional brand, with distribution in drugstores and supermarkets in the Northeast, Mid-Atlantic, and West Coast. We've decided to build our business more intensely in those regions by getting our deodorant and mouthwash into distribution along with our toothpaste instead of using limited resources to become a national toothpaste company.

Our diversity also protects us against competitive threats. Another company might be able to fight us for the toothpaste market, but it would be a lot tougher—and more expensive—to outmarket us as a brand if we're selling mouthwash and deodorant along with toothpaste. We've defended our place in the market by going beyond the product as our only reason for existence. Not only are we committed to profiting from a natural product, we're also benefiting from Tom's of Maine's all-out commitment to social responsibility. It is now harder to knock off Tom's of Maine. Consequently, we can grow the company naturally without the need to make quick moves into the national market by borrowing money and losing family control.

We are now on the verge of a new media strategy that will use, for the first time, newspaper, magazine, and television ads that will be loaded with information about what's in our products and why, as well as an account of the company's beliefs and Mission. We will offer free samples through an 800-number and be involved in sponsoring local groups that help the needy and the environment. It's all more complex than the simple radio spots we've used in the past, but it's also more beautiful and excellent. It's complexity that comes right out of our Mission:

 To be a profitable and successful company, while acting in a socially and environmentally responsible manner.

This is no simple message; it is, in fact, a revolutionary way to do business. But the beauty of the Mission, and its power, comes from its complexity. Managing for profit and for the common good is not a simple notion; nor is our commitment, as the Mission also states, "to build a relationship with our customers that extends beyond product usage to include full and honest dialogue." Complexity and diversity are at the center of the identity of Tom's of Maine. That's why we pursue it in every area of our business.

THE COMPANY AS
A DIVERSE ECOSYSTEM

In his wonderful book *The Diversity of Life,* to which I referred earlier as having been key to catalyzing my commitment to diversity, Edward O. Wilson illustrates the ecosystem of the rain forest by describing what happens when loggers cut down so many trees that they leave a gaping hole in dense, leafy, green cover—the canopy—of the forest. The new light shining on the floor of the forest soon changes the ecosystem dramatically. Insects or a species of animal in the area who were dependent upon the moist ground or darkness may now be damaged or wiped out by the intense sun; other species that depend on the presence of those life-forms will be soon affected too. The entire ecosystem, simply because of the disappearance of a few trees, is thrown into disarray; shifts are made; ways of restoring the balance and replenishing what is missing have to be found. The nature of things is changed, perhaps forever.

Just as scientists like Wilson teach us about how ecosystems live in balance with one another, we have to learn how companies, too, can work to balance their own internal and external diverse "ecosystems" of human interrelationships, gifts, talents, abilities, and complaints.

I am convinced that a company cannot be too diverse. There is no human or spiritual limit. We have not yet even seen the horizon. We have certainly not learned everything there is to know about fairness and justice. Nor have we mastered combining the complexity of power on the one hand with humility on the other—the paradoxical traits embodied in the great figures of Christ and Buddha. Diversity is a complex beauty, but it is also the affirmation of the different gifts we all bring to the table. Diversity is part of our interdependence, broadening our tolerance and our understanding that we are not in a larger sense powerful and indispensable. Just as we need other people in our personal lives, we need others in business too. We are like the denizens of one vast rain forest, dependent on every tiny insect and leaf for our lives. Therein lies the balance to the system.

Unlike life in the rain forest, however, we CEOs have a choice about how we survive in the jungles of business. Our diversity is not forced upon us by nature; we can manage our diversity and set goals. We can take the initiative to change the way we are, to choose to be different. What holds all these differences together is the way in which we, like life in the rain forest, learn to adjust and live in balance with one another.

In 1992 I actually spent a few days walking through a Brazilian rain forest. It is like nothing else you've ever experienced. You see green upon green, brown trunks and brown limbs—and then suddenly you come upon one beautiful, rare flower, tall, pointing straight toward heaven, stunning in its vibrant, natural, and isolated beauty.

My dream is for Tom's of Maine to be that rare beauty standing in the midst of diversity, part of it, feeding off it, growing from it, seeding it, and shining forth as an example of what can be.

How to Create Diversity
and Honor It—In Yourself
and Others

The single most important factor in achieving diversity is the attempt. You have to try. Hard. You must be absolutely intentional. You have to create opportunities to discover your own "variety of gifts" as well as those of others. Here are some specific tips that I have learned while trying to see the complex beauty of the different:

1. CEOs must value taking a walk off their customary paths of power. Leave your CEO persona behind, and get involved more as a human being outside the office, either in family relationships or in your community, church, or other organizations.

2. Seek out organizations where you are likely to come into contact with your "alter ego"—not the power brokers you live among daily but the *powerless,* the oppressed. Go to those outside the cycle of opportunity and success and ask them what they need, and I guarantee that you will not be able to turn them down. I also guarantee that you will learn things about yourself that you never knew before, things that will change your life. (If you go merely with a checkbook in hand, you won't learn a damn thing except how conceited you are.)

3. Be absolutely diligent about bringing diversity into the company. New people, different people, from different backgrounds, with different perspectives on life, will invigorate your company.

4. Try to be inclusive in your organization. When you organize teams or committees or work groups, make sure different perspectives are included in each. The same old people will give you the same old answers. In other words, *create circles* that include a variety of "gifts."

5. Listen to what your associates, staff, and employees have to say. Work at it. It's not as easy as it sounds. But by sharing more of who you are and your rationale on the problem at hand, you are likely to find out more about what's on their minds. Reveal yourself more humanly to the people who work for you. Try to be more than a walking job category. By being a deep listener, you will soon discover that the answers you need are all around you.

6. Humility teaches us that we're not all perfect. Wholeness lies in our interrelations with others. You don't need to have all the answers if you can count on the gifts of someone in the circle.

7. Work hard at figuring out how to create procedures in your company that will facilitate solution—ways to encourage your employees to offer their ideas and apply their creativity, energy, and vision to every cause.

8. Affirm your teammates for their small steps as well as their big steps. They need to know that you believe in them.

9. Above all, be prepared to be surprised. Allowing diversity to flourish is likely to produce results that are different from the ones you originally envisioned. Count on those results being better.

III

INTEGRATING VALUES, BELIEFS, and BUSINESS

8

AUTONOMY: FREEDOM IN SERVICE

Within the past year or so, three of our major competitors—three really big boys—came calling. The conversations went something like, "You're doing well. We like what you're doing. We'd like to buy your business."

It was very flattering. But my answer was, "No way!" They wondered if there was some kind of "strategic alliance" we could work out. I've been around long enough to know that "strategic alliance" is simply another way of saying, "We won't buy you now, but we will get you committed, and down the road you'll have no choice but to sell." I turned them all down—no sale today, thank you.

But as I said, it was flattering. It's nice to get asked to the dance even if you'd rather stay home and read Jonathan Edwards. Periodically, we get such a knock on the door; it's always fascinating to see how others view your company, particularly the huge corporations whose annual advertising budgets add up to more than Tom's of Maine's annual sales. It's fun to hear the questions they ask.

"What is the position 'community life,' and what does it do?" a recent representative of a large consumer packaged-goods multinational asked. Colleen explained that she works with the employees to find ways that we can all live our corporate mission; outside the company, she selects local community groups and nonprofit organizations whose efforts align with our corporate mission for grants. Impressed, the representative described his own company's mission. It was my turn to be impressed, though their mission said nothing about the environment.

Afterward, I wondered what life—and business—would be like if Tom's of Maine were under the tutelage of a large American corporation. What if I had walked into the chairman's office and told him that I would still like to be president of his subsidiary, but that for the next four years I intended to run the company from a pay phone in the basement of a classroom building of the Harvard Divinity School? What if I asked my corporate parent to let me create a position like vice-president of community life and to hire a woman who had no experience in corporate life, but a master's of divinity degree? What if I explained to my new bosses that one of the tasks of the department of community life was to give away $150,000 to community groups? Would I still be president of their subsidiary after I explained that Tom's employees should be spending part of their *paid* time working as volunteers for local projects to help the needy?

Before showing me the door, I suspect the president of the operating unit of this multibillion-dollar behemoth would point out that $150,000 is more than enough to launch new Tom's of Maine products, or to test the power of television in a selected market share—two projects that have been on hold for a while now at Tom's for lack of time and money.

Happily, I have been able to do all of the above because Tom's is *my* company. My wife and I and our family have controlled more than 50 percent of the stock from day one. Our original attorney, Fred Scribner, even wiser now in his eighties, instilled in us from the start the importance of controlling the stock. The main reason: autonomy—a word that literally means "self-rule." It's a kind of freedom, a complicated kind of freedom that quite simply has allowed me to transform both myself and Tom's of Maine.

Who doesn't want to be completely free? I'm not talking about being free to do whatever you damned well please. Even entrepreneur-CEOs like myself and others who control the stock of a company are still accountable to a board of directors and shareholders. The kind of freedom I'm talking about is much more interesting and paradoxical than a simple license to do what you please. What I have in mind, and what I've tried to instill in Tom's of Maine, is the *freedom to serve*. That, in my opinion, is the ultimate freedom: to use your freedom—and this is the paradox—to be locked into the service of others, *bound to them* in your shared concern for your good and their good—the common good.

Without this kind of autonomy, there is no morality. Freedom rests at the core of the moral corporation—the freedom to serve others. The business leader who can take the freedom he has as the head of a company and transmit it to his executives and employees—integrate it into his business strategy—will have reimagined the essence of his business. No longer will he be at the head of a company managed by fear and second-guessing. Creativity and innovation—freedom's children—will reign.

BREAKING THE CHAIN

I've made three major breaks for freedom in my business career. The first was when I quit the confines of Aetna to find a job that allowed me more self-expression. The second was when I walked out of my own father's office and slammed the door on two years of trying to work with the man who has always meant the most to me. The break from Aetna was easy compared to the anguish of ending my father's dream to be partners with his son. But like my father, I was an entrepreneur, and I had to make a go of it on my own. (Disappointed as he was, my father encouraged me. He and my mother have retired and now live in Kennebunk. I still consider him my model of passion, courage, and responsibility.) My third move into the fresh air was the decision to go to divinity school.

In divinity school I was finally able to sort out my ambivalence about how to handle freedom, with the help of Saint Paul and Immanuel Kant. "Autonomy," Kant explained, can be divided into two kinds of freedom—"freedom from" something (Aetna, my father, the calculations of my young MBAs) and "freedom to" do something else. In First Corinthians Saint Paul talks about service as a kind of freedom. Once Paul was converted to Christianity, he realized he could do nothing else but try to convert others to this new moral law that he had embraced so passionately. "I have no choice but to preach the gospel," said Paul.

So as I began to transform Tom's of Maine in the early 1990s— once we started to live the Mission—I understood better in practical, business terms what Kant and Saint Paul were talking about. As an entrepreneur controlling my own profitable company, I was *free from* the corporate rat race, but for such autonomy to become meaningful and fulfilling, I would have to serve others—my customers, my employees, our communities. In Kant's terms, I was *free to* serve the common good. It was a choice, and it was in my own free will to make it.

One of the most important messages we entrepreneurs can bring to the business world at large is that freedom from all constraint is only a temporary joy. Creating your own business, making it a success, and walking down the street with your pockets filled with the money from your megabuyout are bound to be satisfying. But not for long. No matter how much money you have or how much free time, the question nags, "What's next? How do I find meaning in the rest of my life?"

THE DUTIES OF FREEDOM

Most people tend to think of absolute freedom as the absence of all constraints, to be free to do what they want, to let it rip. But as an entrepreneur free to make my ideas and dreams come true, I've learned that the most rewarding kind of freedom is *responsibility*—the duty to help others and the community. Yes, I am free to run my own company; yes, I am free to choose to be innovative. But if I want to create a moral and socially responsible company, if I want to manage for the common good as well as for profit, then I have to be responsible to all the people who make my business possible. It was Jonathan Edwards's notion of "being is relation" all over again. No moral leader is free to do what he wants because morality, by definition, is about how what you do affects others.

I was free but, paradoxically, free to serve others.

POWER VERSUS AUTHORITY

In the past few years, as I have been trying to establish autonomy at the core of Tom's of Maine, I have learned that there's a big difference between power and authority. In most corporate hierarchies power and authority seem to be pretty much the same thing. Power rises to the top of the corporate pyramid, and those at the top have all the authority. At Tom's, authority is still at the top of the pyramid, ultimately in the hands of the board of directors and the shareholders. But the power at Tom's of Maine is *shared*. We have tried to create an interdepartmental company where managers discuss their problems and offer their solutions in the equality of the circle: Every executive has the power to innovate.

But no one has absolute power. As I said in my discussion of the triangle and circle in chapter 7, shared power is not something that happens on its own. Those in authority must step back and allow the creative powers of their managers to emerge or develop. It is no easy decision for any leader to give up wielding power. Even after divinity school opened my eyes to the power of doing good, of diversity, of dialogue in the circle, of the management riches of autonomy, I held on to my control over the company—my power—as greedily as any petty potentate.

EMPOWERING YOUR MANAGERS

"Autonomy is fine for you, Tom, because you're at the top of the pyramid," Ruth Purtilo said to me one day, catching me a bit off guard. A member of the Tom's of Maine board, Ruth is a medical ethicist who brings a fresh perspective to our business from the outside. "What's it like for others in the hierarchy?" she asked. I still wasn't quite sure what she meant, but Ruth couldn't have been more candid: "Do you and your managers grant others in the company the freedom to serve?" she asked.

It was a profound question. Truth was, not only had I been reluctant to sell Tom's of Maine, I had kept the managing control of the company right in my lap. Even after Tom's had grown beyond a family company to one with professionals running both the sales and marketing departments, neither of those executives could make a move without me. By the time Ruth blindsided me with her question, I was well into my re-creation of the company; the Mission was three years under way. I felt that I had definitely grown a great deal as a leader, but her question still stopped me short. I was reveling in my own freedom to create a new kind of socially responsible American company, but had I transmitted the teachings of autonomy to my key managers?

The Mission, after all, was permission for them to manage by values, not by Tom's personal preferences. But to turn over power, I would have to trust my managers. Did I? To explore the issue of trust at Tom's and how we could share power, we organized a management retreat to try to see what we expected in our hierarchical relations at Tom's of Maine and what we were actually getting.

THE TRUST FACTOR

"What do I need to bring me to trust someone else?" "How can I actually build trust in someone I'm working with?" These were the two main questions that I and fifteen members of my management team addressed as we broke up into small groups amid the natural beauty of Cushing, on Maine's midcoast. We began to admit to each other that we weren't always the trustworthy souls we thought ourselves to be. Sometimes we worked with our own secret agendas; other times we were just plain unfair to our colleagues. We began to see that if we were going to build trust companywide, we had to be more careful in our relationships with one another, a little more sensitive.

At one point, each person in the circle was invited to tell a story about a personal experience of trust. Kate described the shock of finding out that one of our suppliers had lied to us about the ingredients in a flavor. We had thought it was natural, but the harder we pressed to find out exactly what was in it, the less willing the supplier was to level with us. Finally, we found out that the flavor had one ingredient that was not natural. We discontinued our relationship with that company. Its other flavors were truly natural, but we no longer could trust it.

David, a purchasing executive who's been with the company for more than a decade, told a story about how he and I had planned a sailing trip with our sons on my boat. Two days before we were scheduled to leave, I was summoned to jury duty. David recalled that instead of canceling the trip, I told him to take the boat and the kids, mine included, and have a great time. Apparently, David had been moved by my willingness to trust him with both my boat and children. I had almost forgotten the incident; at the time it was no big deal. David was an experienced sailor. I trusted him.

By the end of this session, we realized that it takes faith to trust someone. The building blocks of trust are listening and honesty. Trust is a rather fragile commodity; as soon as you see someone taking advantage of your goodwill, it vanishes.

We now had a new perspective on the diagram I drew years before of "the free and responsible corporation."

Kate redubbed this interlocking web of circles "The Wheel of Trust." It helped us all see that building trust in each of these corporate relationships must be a primary goal of the kind of socially responsible company that Tom's of Maine was trying to be.

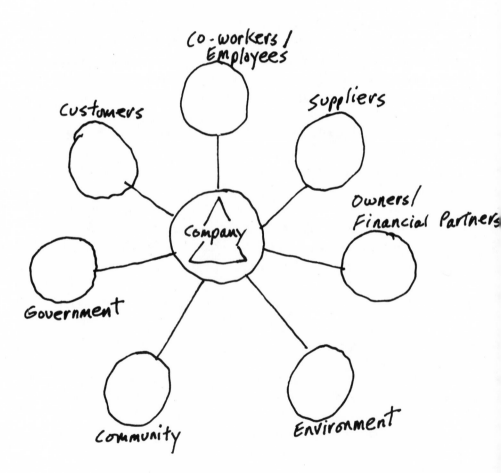

I set out to pass along my power to them—not to give up my authority as CEO and controlling shareholder but to encourage them to think for themselves and to be as free as I was to serve our customers, the community, and nature in the most responsible ways possible. I wanted to *empower* the other leaders of Tom's of Maine. But I also wanted them to discover that in that power was their duty to serve others. How could I convey this not-so-traditional idea that the good businessperson must not exploit or trick consumers into buying his products but actually *serve* them?

One afternoon while I was on vacation, something slightly outrageous occurred to me. After I give a speech or at social occasions, people have a curious habit of coming up to me to talk about my products. "I was thinking about you this morning as I brushed my teeth and put on my deodorant," they'll say, and without so much as a blush, they'll begin talking about their everyday relationship to Tom's of Maine—in the privacy of their own bathroom, in God knows what state of undress. In my next meeting with my creative team in R&D and marketing, I explained my idea of service in the following way:

> When you're developing a product or packaging it or writing copy for it, I want you to imagine yourself talking to someone—a customer—who is standing absolutely naked in his or her bathroom. They are in as vulnerable a state as anybody could be. They bought your product, they trust you, and they're going to use it in that state of absolute vulnerability. Naked. And you're the only people who can determine the safety, efficacy, and total integrity of that product in that moment.

I informed those executives that if they couldn't answer these criteria in their decisions about product development, packaging, or copy, then they hadn't served the customer. We all had to be intentional about establishing trust, both with our customers and among ourselves. Trust can be contagious. I worked hard at creating trust between me and my managers, and once they sensed that I trusted them, freedom began to flow down through the hierarchy; creativity, innovation, and passion soon followed.

LET FREEDOM RING!: TWO EXAMPLES
OF THE POWER OF AUTONOMY

FREEDOM TO ANTICIPATE PROBLEMS: CHET

The prime beneficiary of power-sharing at Tom's of Maine was bound to be Chet, the executive vice-president in charge of finance and manufacturing. My own passions were R&D, marketing, and sales. I had made my share of deals with banks and overseen the finances as well as manufacturing for fifteen years before Chet, an experienced professional accountant, joined the company in 1985. But this area was definitely not my prime interest. From the start, Chet has been a self-starter. His judgment is impeccable, and he is sensitive to the day-to-day problems of production efficiency and quality. He also has a knack for keeping our banking relations as well oiled as the machines down at the plant.

In the mid-1980s, as small banks were collapsing around the country or being acquired by larger ones, Chet raised the possibility that we should switch our banking relationship away from the small institution I had been banking with for five years. We queried our banker on how his operation was holding up, and he assured us that it was rock solid. Chet was not as sanguine, however, and began calling around to his long-standing financial contacts in the Boston area for an alternative. Within three months our "rock solid" bank's financial business proved to be severely wounded. Chet made a phone call, and within a week we were hooked into a private bank that he had already talked to. (It didn't hurt that some of the bank's partners were Tom's of Maine customers.) Within a month our old bank went under.

Chet had grabbed the ball and run with it: *He* had raised the concern about the stability of the bank, *he* had found an alternative, and when the time came, *he* had made the switch, without so much as a tremor in the financial stability of Tom's of Maine. At a time when banks were calling in loans all over the country and when commercial credit was tight, Chet had placed us in a secure financial relationship.

Chet has also taken control over the engineering side of the business. When it came time to invest a million dollars in new production equipment—a huge amount of money for a small company like ours—Chet empowered the new engineering team to handle the purchase, which they did, creatively and cost-efficiently. Tom's of Maine replaced its old equipment with a stainless-steel, high-speed manufacturing, filling, and packaging machine for both our toothpaste and our deodorant. With the same number of people working on a shift, the new equipment has allowed us to *more than double* our production. Today, output is up to 48,000 units per shift compared with 20,000 on the old equipment. I had nothing to do with it except admire the results and pat myself on the back for hiring Chet.

This kind of empowerment keeps flowing down the line, as one person's autonomy encourages another's. Gary Rittershaus, the head of manufacturing whom Chet had brought over from the quality assurance department, began experimenting with ways of reforming the hierarchy of the production process. Taking the teachings of the Mission to heart and knowing that Chet encourages innovation, Gary took the initiative to set up interdepartmental circles between the quality assurance and production departments. The happy result: Both departments were able to suggest ways of integrating their functions so that the entire production-quality assurance process became more efficient and thus more productive. It was Chet, too, who recognized that the former production manager's experience would transfer laterally into a new position for safety concerns.

FREEDOM TO DECIDE: COLLEEN

Power is intoxicating to a CEO; so is a big title, and the office and salary that go with it. But none of these bestows infallibility. I've found that if you give people the freedom to prove you wrong, you'll eventually recognize that you're not omniscient; morale is likely to improve as well as productivity. Not long ago, Colleen informed me that one of her new recruits had requested that the company send him to Russia for two weeks to attend a conference to help educate emerging Russian and Eastern European businesses in organizational theory. Concluding that the Moscow seminar was consistent with the Mission "to address community concerns, in Maine and around the globe," Colleen approved the trip.

I was concerned that a manager who'd been with Tom's of Maine for only four months was hardly ready to promote the values of the company. Colleen clarified that Stephen was attending the Moscow conference to discuss not our company but what he had learned from his previous job in human resource management for a large New England manufacturer. Stephen would be, she said, a kind of donation from Tom's of Maine. She assured me he would return with information that would be valuable in his work.

I wasn't so sure. But it was Colleen's judgment call, and I told her so. Stephen returned from Moscow with a great deal to share with us about the struggle for profit and responsibility as Russia and Eastern Europe plunged into free-market economies. Colleen had been right, and I've told her so.

Trust-building can be painful and is often filled with conflict. Perspectives are bound to differ. We may have our intuitions, but they will not always converge. We at Tom's continue to work through the processes that lead to trust, however, and beneath the conflicts and disagreements lies our mutual respect.

EARNING TRUST

Kate and I have grown up in business together. We've had our business conflicts and shouting matches. But now we're in sync. We can stand in each other's shoes. Same with Chet. We started out at opposite ends of a forty-foot conference table; I knew I needed his financial talent, but I wanted to keep my distance. Today, we sit elbow to elbow, anticipating each other's responses, finishing each other's sentences. He's become my alter ego, the man who runs the business when I'm unavailable. Our lives in business together have become truly symbiotic.

Relationships like this one are truly special—in business they are hard to come by. Trust must be built. Katie Shisler has my full trust in dealing with human relationships. She is driven by the Mission and has transmitted this passion to Heidi, the communications manager, who oversees consumer mail, media relations, and the company sponsorships. From the hundreds of requests we get for help, Heidi and her assistant in public relations, Brian, select the five percent of groups that we give money to. These people are on fire with the Mission. On their own they go out and find the best groups. When I made Katie head of marketing, I got a department full of communicators. They can tell the Tom's of Maine story as well as I can.

But when it comes to the content of that story, the selection of the media, and the total communications strategy, I have kept that responsibility. Katie and I collaborate on the content and she manages the communications strategy, but I have the first—and last—word on how Tom's of Maine is presented to the public. This is the heart of the business, and it will take years of working with someone before I ever delegate it. What gets said to the customer and what gets put into those products is *the soul* of the company, and it will take years of working with someone before I delegate it. That will take time. The kind of mutual respect Katie and I have suggests that we are on our way to the kind of special business relationship I already have with Kate and Chet.

I have also not given up my control over the brand—what I call "the architecture of the brand." You *build* a brand like a house. We've been a toothpaste company, but we have to build the house of personal care—toothpaste plus mouthwash, floss, deodorant, soaps, shampoos. You have to design all this carefully—then know when to go back and renovate other parts of the structure (like adding a baking soda toothpaste and then a children's toothpaste and then giving the brand a boost with a new natural deodorant). You can never leave your properties unattended.

As much as I value autonomy and empowering my employees, I

recognize that you cannot delegate everything. Some gifts are not immediately transferable. If I hired a brand architect, what would it add to the company but unnecessary conflict? Instead, I've designed my executive team around the company's existing "gifts."

That's not to say that I'm not ready to stand corrected. Over the past two decades, I've learned a lot about how to sell the company to the public and build the brand; I've also learned a few things about the value of humility at the top.

HUMILITY:

AUTONOMY'S SECRET WEAPON

Humility is a virtue not much discussed in American business schools. Young executives lust for power and control; older executives use their power to hammer their subordinates into submission. Any executive who admitted that he was practicing humility would either be pushed off the fast track or sent off for psychiatric observation. Humility, however, does have a distinguished tradition in religious thought. The Latin word *humilitas* has its roots literally in the ground—having evolved from the Latin *humus,* which means "ground." Originally meaning "lowly," *humilitas* eventually came to mean "the absence of pride or assertion" and thus our own sense of "humble." In the Judeo-Christian tradition, humility became a saintly quality. In the Catholic and Episcopal churches, priests are ordained lying prone on the floor before their bishops as a sign of their humility and willingness to enter God's service. In many religions humility is a major virtue, one that even the most powerful of men ought to cultivate. In fact, two of the greatest figures in the history of religion—Christ and Buddha—combine majesty with humility.

I have learned that a business leader can be truly powerful only when he's humble. After all, we are in business to serve customers and to serve them well. We must also serve our employees—how else will we be able to make money? The Christian tradition that I've been raised and educated in teaches that life is a "gift" from God—we are in this life as God's guests, as it were. We each have particular gifts to be used, not for our own sake but for the sake of others. People like myself who have grown up in an affluent culture, who've had a wonderful education, and who've made it to the top of the corporate pyramid, or whose companies, like Tom's of Maine, have achieved visibility on the shelves equal to huge brands, have accumulated considerable power along their successful journey.

Personally, I don't value that kind of power, unless I'm able to share it or use it as a means to make life richer for other people. In that sense, my function in life is to be part of someone else's story—a player in my wife Kate's world, in our children's, in my board of directors', in my employees'. I serve them. I stand with them, contributing my gifts to them; we are in a partnership, a joint venture, a co-creation. In a very real sense I am their *disciple;* they are mine.

I know that sounds strange coming from a CEO. Most business leaders would say "I manage my employees" or "I control them" or, more bluntly, "My people don't make a move without authorization from me." That's not what I'm about. Unfortunately, we live in a society where there's too little real autonomy. It's very hard to teach what it means to serve until you've been free. The irony is that once you get free, you want to be who you are. You can't justify your life by having only what you want. You justify your life by using your gifts to make someone else's life easier. Generally, people believe their worthiness stands on how great they've become, how rich or famous. But real worthiness evolves from having sacrificed your time, money, and talents to build up someone who's weaker than you are, who needs your help, who needs your money. A real business leader seeks his worthiness among his employees. I visit my employees; I talk to them; I find out what's going on in their lives. I'm one of them. I stand with them.

I also act as *their voice.*

PASSIONATE WORK: THE RIGHT TO BE AS FREE AS THE COMPANY PRESIDENT

When I discovered that the reason we were having trouble employing receptionists and people in the mailroom was that their boss was mistreating them, I fired him. I won't stand for abusive authority or insensitivity. If people can't treat others with respect at Tom's of Maine, I want them the hell out! I'll intervene, and I'll get their ass out of there. I've done it more than once. I want people at Tom's of Maine to have a voice. Free to speak, to make suggestions. I want my employees to be heard.

Autonomy is having a voice no matter what your education level, your job status, or the neighborhood you grew up in. You have a right to tell your boss how you feel. As a high school and college student, I had summer jobs working in textile mills during the second shift, alongside men and women who worked too hard (occasionally drank too hard) and were paid too little. Those people, too, needed a voice, and remembering them in my current lofty position, I want to speak for my workers. The best leaders, those most comfortable with their authority and their power, will be eager to step down from the top of the pyramid and see what the company looks like from the ground. Humility is about being able to take your ego and stick it in your desk drawer.

Yet no one was more reluctant than I to yield power. Even when I thought I had become one of the most magnanimous CEOs in the land, Ruth Purtilo reminded me that my view of autonomy might not be the same as that of my executives or employees. But, I will assure you, employees with autonomy who have a share in the company's power, are the most passionate and creative workers you will ever find. By saying that autonomy comes first at Tom's of Maine, we have said that we value our right to be creative and innovative—to solve problems as each one of us sees fit. I look at the consumer mail department, where Ronda is begging for more staff, but my budget tells me I have to put the money into other departments. Occasionally, I catch myself wondering whether there is an ideal form letter out there that can convey the kind of intimacy appropriate to Tom's but keep Ronda's assistants from spending two hours answering a particularly persnickety customer.

But then in my mind I hear Ronda's voice repeating, "There will never be a form letter sent out from Tom's of Maine so long as I'm in charge of this department!" in a tone of voice that makes it clear that a form letter from a company with our beliefs would be heresy. When Ronda answers a consumer complaint, she has the freedom to act as if she were the president of Tom's of Maine—and she is free to be candid.

This is how you get passion, how you motivate your employees If I lorded it over Ronda, ignored her ideas, dumped on her innovations, would she be as motivated as she is every day, or would I have a resentful, sullen employee on my hands? I prefer the passion.

Recently, I was meeting with three of my top executives about a proposal to make free samples of toothpaste available through an 800-number—something we had never done before. My managers were bogged down in the figures, wondering whether dispersing trial sizes of toothpaste through an 800-number would be cost-efficient; they discussed the alternatives. I couldn't believe it. Our focus group research with Ed McCabe had shown that customers were eager to get the free samples quickly and simply, and they loved the idea of a new Tom's of Maine 800-number. So why not go with it and figure out how to make it work efficiently as we went along?

I didn't want anyone to suffocate an original idea in spreadsheets. I stopped them. "I'm not interested in your calculations about what's affordable," I said. "I want to know your passions. Speak with your heart!" I told them that for our next meeting I wanted them to go out and buy a large pitcher and bring it along. In the center of the circle, I told them, there will be a large basin. "When you're speaking from your heart and with passion," I informed my surprised colleagues, "I want you to pour water from the pitcher into the bowl, as if you were pouring your own essence into it." I figured that when they were speaking about something they truly believed in and were excited about, standing there, pitcher in hand, wouldn't faze them one bit. But if they were just mouthing expediencies, that pitcher would feel pretty odd and make them conscious of their lack of enthusiasm for their idea.

I explained that I didn't want rational analysis; I wanted them to talk about what they desired most. "I'm not interested in your calculations about what's affordable," I told them. "I can get the numbers from any executive in America with a pocket calculator." From my own top executives, the people to whom I'm entrusting the future of my company, I want great ideas and creativity, and only passion produces that. I want to know what presses the budget to the wall. I want answers that are based on what's responsible, fair, and reasonable in a relationship. Bonds, not safe calculations. I want more than their analysis; I want their essence in the bowl.

FREEDOM ALSO MEANS
ACCOUNTABILITY

By demanding passion, I am hardly giving my managers license to swerve out of control. Autonomy is not about the freedom to go crazy. There are limits, and they're set by *accountability*. No matter how much Ronda thinks she needs more staff, she also must know that the CEO is as concerned about the company's financial health as she is about its customers. She also needs to know that her zeal may be matched by the engineering department's desire to produce a better product for which it needs a new piece of equipment that costs $500,000. In other words, Ronda needs to listen, too, and see things from the perspective of the whole company.

Autonomy can be structured. At Tom's we're striving to help each employee know they are free but that autonomy begins with agreed-upon objectives that are constantly being clarified. At the beginning of every creative enterprise we are bound to muddle around; one executive may step on another's toes; but eventually an idea will emerge. I'll expect to hear about your progress, and you'll bounce that idea off of me or another executive. You're accountable to us; we're accountable to someone else. From the outset I expect Tom's of Maine employees to keep the values of the company at the forefront; no matter how brilliant an idea might be, if it doesn't fit with the Mission, it's not going to fly.

Some might consider the Mission to be a curb on their freedom, but in another sense it is liberating. As soon as employees recognize that an idea is a natural for the Mission, they can pull out all stops, as

Chet, Colleen, and Katie do every day. If I'm away and a decision has to be made, I know I can trust my management team to make it. That's not to say we won't disagree, but we'll be able to talk about it. My managers all know where the final authority rests. They are free to pursue their objectives, but they know that it's their responsibility to keep me informed. I get regular monthly reports from each department, I know what kind of shrinkage is occurring in manufacturing, I know how well our customers are paying us, I know where our sales come from geographically, I know what specific items are sold, and I know our financial result, all on a monthly basis. Part of my responsibility is to pay attention to this flow of information so that I can help my managers manage. We have regular conversations. They are free, I hope, from my tampering. But they are not free from their accountability to me. If I disagree, I will tell them. If I find their objectives wrongheaded, I will let them know—sometimes loudly.

I can get very angry. It's not something I'm proud of. My managers and employees will be the first to tell you that I've been known to yell. But they also know me as a complex person. I'm very competitive; I'm just as eager to win in the marketplace and come home with a big profit as any capitalist. But what saves me, I think (and hope), is that I care deeply about the people I work with. I care deeply about raising the standard of living in the town I live in. If one of my employees hasn't enough money to put food on the table that week, or has had a death in the family, or has a health problem, I want them to know they can depend on me for assistance. You don't need a policy to help someone out.

I'm even prouder of the fact that employees can depend on the other top executives at Tom's of Maine too. I remember not long ago when a young worker was regularly having temper tantrums, verbally abusing fellow workers day in and day out. The employee's superiors were on the verge of making the discharge decision when the employee revealed, "I've got a drinking problem." The supervisors replied, "That's something we didn't know," and then said that if the employee were willing to follow a doctor's orders, the company would be supportive. The employee agreed. We helped this person

175

get into Alcoholics Anonymous, and the employee is still working for us, while working to get life in general back into shape.

Another company might not have been so understanding. In the traditional utilitarian calculus, a problem employee can't be given the benefit of the doubt and has to be sacrificed for the happiness of the rest of the company. But that's not the way of Tom's of Maine. At the core of our value system is the principle of love of neighbor; bonds between people must be respected. Our managers are encouraged to put themselves in another person's shoes. I know they care about communities and the people using our products. They care about the family lives of Tom's of Maine employees—as much as they care about R&D, manufacturing, company finances, and profit margins. So they will honor the company's bond to an employee enough to say, "We'll help you out even if you've broken every damned rule in the place—if you're willing to try to pull yourself together."

THE RISKS OF AUTONOMY

In a sense, that's what we're all trying to do every day—pull ourselves together. It's certainly what I was trying to do when I interrupted my full-time control of Tom's of Maine to attend divinity school. While I've found my way, I don't pretend I've reached perfection, either as a manager or as a person. We CEOs are models, whether we like it or not. I like to think that I stand before my employees as a symbol of entrepreneurial success, someone who had an idea, gave it a shot, and achieved something worthwhile. More important, I hope they see me as a model of imperfection, someone with high ideals definitely, but still a man who often falls short.

Autonomy is about that too—a license to make mistakes, to fail sometimes. Autonomy is about taking risks. If you have high ideals, you become a lightning rod for criticism. Conserving autonomy requires turning down some tempting offers. At almost $20 million in sales, we are still a dinghy floating in the water next to the tankers of consumer packaged-goods giants like Bristol-Myers, Johnson &

Johnson, Procter & Gamble. (To play in their game, we would probably need $100 million in annual sales.)

"You don't seem to be in any hurry to get to your new markets,"
commented one of our recent corporate suitors. "Aren't you afraid
some other marketer with money and infrastructure will take your
opportunity away?" Yes, I am afraid of that. But what can I do about
it? I certainly have no control over the strategies of my competitors,
and I know what I will lose if I sell a controlling interest to a brand
marketer. "We deal with the things we can control," I told him, "such
as protecting our freedom."

Recently, our regional sales manager in the Northwest, who had
been working for us for only fifteen months, paid his second visit to
the Tom's of Maine headquarters in Kennebunk. "This is a whole new
company!" he said to his boss.

We're working at it.

HOW TO MANAGE AUTONOMY

Like everything else at Tom's of Maine, the following list is not carved in stone. It is rather a synthesis of my own thoughts over the past few years of trying to manage differently. The very nature of autonomy is to be flexible, creative, free. If a particular principle doesn't work, modify it or toss it out. Consider these ideas as guides for your own discussions about how to empower your employees, from the top of your company right down to the bottom.

- Define your corporate values; make them operate in decisions

- Teach your employees to think, reason, and act in responsible relation to others—customers, fellow workers, bosses, community, and the environment.

- Listen, reflect, share, and clarify. Job roles should be clearly defined. Whenever confusion arises, talk about it.

- Build diverse points of view into the process of setting goals and objectives. Encourage genuine dialogue, welcoming differences of opinion. Diversity also belongs in your formalized systems of accountability.

- Use authority to guide, clarify, and affirm the power of others. Also use it to modify behavior that is controlling, domineering, or manipulative—or terminate it, if necessary.

- Be yourself. Be willing to change when the feedback fits.

- Be understanding when you and others make mistakes.

MANAGING—

AND COMPETING—BY

THE MIDDLE WAY

At a recent meeting of the Tom's of Maine board of directors, Colin Blaydon, a former dean of Dartmouth's Amos Tuck School of Business, asked his fellow board members, "Are we going to remain a lifestyle company in which Tom and Kate govern kindly over their kingdom, or are we going to claim our rightful share of the personal-care business in America?"

It was a tough question. The company had once again reached a crossroads. Our gradual growth on the West Coast, market by market, had boosted our sales toward $20 million, signaling to our competitors that it was time for someone to buy us out. No sooner had I said "No way!" to their various offers, affirming family control of the company, than rumors began to circulate of natural ingredient brands from our competitors. Church and Bright was already on the shelves with their own Arm & Hammer baking soda toothpaste; Procter & Gamble and Colgate soon responded with their own versions. Johnson & Johnson had plans in the works for a children's toothpaste. Gillette has introduced a new deodorant with lichen, the ingredient whose odor-eating power we discovered. For a decade, Tom's had the only nonalcoholic mouthwash on the market; several other brands are now introducing their first nonalcoholic mouthwashes.

Colin set out the options very clearly. Kate and I could live with an average annual growth of 20 to 25 percent, expanding slowly, market by market, from toothpaste to deodorant, and continue to control the company. Or, as Colin put it, we could "raise the necessary capital to grow the business in leapfrog fashion to $100 million in sales and claim our place in the personal-care business."

Kate was the first to state what many other board members were thinking. "I have concerns about how such a rapid growth to $100 million would offset the culture we've labored to create in living a mission that respects other people's dignity, that respects nature and communities," she said. But she also said she would be reluctant to abandon the company's donations to the community if in an effort to grow, Tom's had to forgo profits. "People and groups are beginning to count on our donations each year," she explained. Other board members supported continued family control. One member reminded us that our company could not compete in a market where giants throw twice our net worth into advertising one brand of deodorant alone; he advised continuing our gradual growth and creating new products to throw our competitors off guard.

The discussion was not about growth for growth's sake. We were searching for the right strategy that would enable the company to make a difference, not just a living. The soul of this company is bigger than our maintaining family control for the sake of a nice Maine lifestyle. In order to achieve our business and social aims, we knew the company needed to be bigger.

As I listened to the debate, I realized that Tom's of Maine was more vulnerable than it ever had been. What competitor wouldn't lust after our projected $20 million in sales that are bound to rise exponentially? We hadn't even launched our new TV and print ads or moved into the Rocky Mountain region, where a hotbed of health-conscious Americans are passionately concerned about the environment. Our competitors were now bent on annihilating Tom's of Maine. To the victor would belong our 2.5 million customers and users.

Today, as I write, Tom's of Maine is up against the wall with only 10 percent growth. Accustomed to 25 percent annual increases, I'm loving the challenge of getting the company back to that kind of growth. For almost six years I have been arguing that the success of the company lies in its capacity to become a new kind of company. I've rejected bids from my major competitors because I didn't want to become them. Instead, I had this revolutionary dream: *I wanted them to become us.* I wanted Tom's to become successful to prove that there is another way of doing business in America—to manage by values, to care about people and the environment, and still to run up and down the court with the big boys and make money. My immediate aim has been the success of my company; my long-term goal is to persuade more and more CEOs to adopt my business style. I want to prove that the principle of maximization is dead. At Tom's we have been willing *to give up* production time to get greater productivity.

I call this management by values "the Middle Way," after the Buddhist notion of taking the path between two extremes—in business terms, those extremes being managing *only* for profit or *only* for the common good. The Middle Way is a route where change is the only constant, a principle that fits the intuitive management style at Tom's of Maine perfectly. The decision to go this Middle Way has been an easy one for me—it's right there in the Mission:

 To be a profitable and successful company, while acting in a socially responsible manner.

This is exactly the principle I had in mind when I set up for the board my long-range objective:

 To become the choice of customers who care about health, the natural world, and their communities.

We want to serve not only the people whom market researchers are now calling the health-concerned. We want to appeal also to those people who care about nature and their communities. Market analysts would never have bothered to count these consumers if companies like Tom's of Maine hadn't proved they were there. They are our people, and I want to be the number-one brand in their homes. We are not going to beat Johnson & Johnson or Gillette by trying to play their game. They would bury us in media dollars. But Tom's of Maine cannot devote itself only to doing good works, either. We are not a church or a foundation. Our ability to do good depends on our success in doing well. To tithe ten percent of our profits, we have to earn them. So our strategy is to go after the customers who share our company's values.

Our best defense, I decided, was our traditional offense—managing for profit *and* for the common good. We had gone from zero to $12.5 million by being ourselves. Three years later, after refining our identity—who and what we were—and committing ourselves even more strongly to the common good, we are heading toward $20 million. My current objective is to aim for $100 million by doing what Tom's of Maine does best: *Be Tom's of Maine*—that is, a company committed to people and the environment.

Can we succeed with this upside-down vision of American capitalism? I don't know for sure. I never have known for sure. But in this part of the book, I'll show you what we're up against. This section has nothing to do with the *history* of Tom's of Maine. I'm writing about the present now, about precisely what the board and management of Tom's of Maine are up against today. And I mean *today*. I've just interrupted this chapter for a phone call with one of my executives about a disagreement on a training program for our executives. A few days ago, I met with Ed McCabe on the new media campaign, and the company is in the midst of a search for a new head of R&D.

As I've mentioned before, Kate and I have done our share of winging it. We're still managing on the run. But no matter the uncertainties, one thing at Tom's of Maine is always for sure: We know what kind of company we are and what our mission is. We've found our Middle Way—managing for profit and for the common good—and it has worked for us.

MANAGING ON THE RUN
IN THE MIDDLE WAY

Businesspeople are always asking me to describe how we manage at Tom's of Maine. "We know what your values and mission are, but how do you put that stuff into practice, in the day-to-day chaos of the office and the marketplace?" It's not easy, mainly because by definition, the Middle Way is about being flexible, not setting anything in stone.

Picture in your mind a management team; now picture them on the run, men and women, jogging down the beach, like in the opening and final scenes of that great movie *Chariots of Fire,* where Britain's Olympic track team of 1927 joyously runs along the shore. That's my management team—instinctive, adaptive, open, interdependent, competitive, and interconnected.

Managing on the run. We are not always exactly sure how we're going to achieve certain objectives, but we pool our strengths, we imagine our way out of our dilemmas, and we come out a winner. We are less managers than *practitioners.* We don't take someone else's knowledge and apply it to our company as "the way to do things." The tried-and-true methods of the business schools are not likely to work for a company eager to temper analysis with social responsibility.

The strengths of our management team are our intuitive and common sense; we play by rules—the instinctive rules of fair play. When one of us is not sure whether a certain move is fair, they know that this very uncertainty signals that it's time for them to discuss things with another member of the executive team. "We've got to be flexible because each of us is different," explains Chet, characterizing our management style. "We listen to one another. Not everyone can go with their gut. We have to play hardball sometimes and draw the line. Like with that piece of equipment we recently had designed for us. They haven't delivered on it, so we're holding back a third of the money. If you tell them, 'No equipment, then no payment,' they respect that and deliver."

We like being winners, but not at all costs. How big is your appetite? Is your only constraint the limits of the law—or the moral law? Tom's of Maine is attempting to succeed according to the principles of the moral law, a harder path to follow and not always as profitable, at least in the short term. But someone in the society has to speak for the disadvantaged and powerless. Some businesses do care about the future of the environment. We want to lead the way—*the Middle Way*.

"A leader finds no resting place on either stand, for the middle way is the only enlightened course," teaches Lao-Tzu's *Tao Te Ching*, the classic *Book of the Way*. The Middle Way is the *practical* path between two values that can often be incompatible—justice versus compassion, profit versus respect. For Buddhists, wisdom and compassion are the two most important values. Happiness, however, lies in the perfection of neither but in finding a middle ground—a middle way—between them. The Middle Way is no theory; it's a practice. I'm not sure you can teach it, but I do know you can do it.

The happy Buddhist is the person who does not promote the absolute value of either wisdom or compassion but who tries to integrate both in his life—wisdom *and* compassion, or in the terms of the Tom's of Maine Mission, profit *and* the common good. "The ferryman goes from shore to the other shore," goes an old Buddhist saying, "but does not stand at either end. Nor does he stand in the great flood."

The Middle Way is not balance, nor is it a kind of compromise. It's a course that keeps in view competing aims: working efficiently versus taking time out for respect; making money versus being kind; having a kick-ass attitude versus having patience. The Middle Way is not "this way" or "that way," either-or; it's *one way that integrates both*. How is it that the Buddha is serene yet mighty? How is it that Christ is meek yet majestic? It's because of how they did things—it's because of the practice of the Middle Way in their lives. The Middle Way is all about the how. The Middle Way is implementing paradoxes on a day-to-day basis. You manage in the equality of the circle within the authority of the triangle. You take two hours off work to celebrate joys and share struggles but also to increase production. You give away your margins to discover more avenues for profit. You make yourself understood by listening to others.

When I interviewed people in my company for this book, I began with a brief description of what I was up to, then sat back and listened for the next hour and a half while employees and executives talked about the company. Inevitably, they would end the meeting with virtually the same comment, "Thank you," they would say. "I really enjoyed this conversation." Those conversations were actually more like monologues, but not only did I end up understanding them and the company better, they understood me better.

Like a boatman navigating a swirling river, Tom's of Maine has to steer between analysis and intuition, between our goals of profit and social responsibility, between softball and hardball. A company can manage this way on the run, in the field of uncertainty, only if its management team has a sense of mutual intimacy. When I invoked that picture of my management team running down the beach together, the implication was that they would stay *together*. You can't have eight people jogging and talking, then suddenly have two of them go off on their own to solve their problems. Some of us are decision-makers and risk-takers; others want to leave the risks and decisions up to others. Some want to be followers; others want to be president. We have to figure out how it all fits together. The company is not an organizational chart but an interdependent system. What you do to the company in one place will have its net effect on it in another place. We have to care about each other as fellow employees, and—absolutely crucial—we have to be interconnected through a good communications system.

The Middle Way belongs to Eastern philosophical views of "relativity." In his introduction to the classic first-century Buddhist text *The Vilmarakirta*, Robert Thurman explains this notion of relativity:

It means that finite things are interdependent, relative and mutually conditioned, and implies that there is no potential of any independent, self-sufficient, permanent thing or entity. An entity exists only in relation to other entities.

Because everything is interconnected—being as well as matter—everything is inseparable. Therefore, the apparent opposites of profit and respect belong together; they are inseparable in any business practice. We twentieth-century businesspeople have to begin to accept the inseparability of human dignity and human utility. They are not opposite poles; it's not all about one or the other; it's not choosing to go to work for a profit as opposed to a nonprofit organization. Happiness is keeping your eye on both sides of the shore; it's having human passion, creativity, and profit. Both extremes are illusions.

Similarly, the executive team is inseparable, a system in itself—marketing, sales, finance, manufacturing, community life, the president's office are all interconnected. Happiness is a practice that we can all believe in. How do you do it? I'm not sure. Each team will accomplish its goals in its own way. You don't try to figure out how they did it; you just stand back and wonder at the results. In the twelve-step theory of recovery for alcohol and drug abusers, you don't try to analyze each step. You just accept that together they got that person straight again. Don't quarrel with the theory; find out if you like the model. Don't debate whether you're in business to make money or to save the world—just do both!

Social scientist Donald A. Schon has written about how the best professionals improvise in their work, about how they seem to know more than what they can put in words. These "reflective practitioners," as Schon calls them in his book of the same name, aren't locked into policies or hard-and-fast rules about "the way things ought to be done." Rather than searching for those elusive universal models that will apply in all situations, Schon suggests,

> let us search, instead, for an epistemology of practice implicit in the artistic, intuitive processes which some practitioners do bring to situations of uncertainty, instability, uniqueness, and value conflict.

This describes Tom's of Maine perfectly: uncertainty, instability, uniqueness, and value conflict. We have it all, and we're also "practitioners" very much in the way that Schon suggests. Our business is so different, we have to make up a lot as we go along. "Our knowing is in our action," just as Schon says. No one technique is available to us; we have to do it and reflect on it at the same time. It's part of the fun of entrepreneurship and managing on the edge of new frontiers. But guiding our intuitions and every move is our Mission to treat every person with dignity, to respect nature as a sacred gift, to contribute as much as we can to the community—and to make a sizable profit to do all of the above.

JUST DOING IT—DAY TO DAY

The Middle Way can be as easy as using local materials or suppliers to support the regional economy. Tom's of Maine gets its paper and a good deal of its glass from New England companies. Only when we can't find something in Maine or New England do we go farther afield. The Middle Way can also be as simple as recycling your wastepaper at the office, something many businesses already do. Tom's alone doesn't generate enough paper to meet the minimum load that our local recycler will pick up, so we've made an arrangement with other groups in the community. They drop their paper at our plant, where the recycler picks it up.

It's a typical Middle Way solution. We couldn't simply pick up the phone and solve our recycling problem; we had to try a few things, talk to other organizations, work it out. The Middle Way is all about action—trial and error—not reflection alone. What works for Tom's of Maine will not necessarily work for you. For your business strategy to be ethical, it must be personal—it must reflect your values, the identity of your company. At Tom's, for example, I fight a constant battle over whether to use glass or recyclable plastic for our roll-on deodorant. The rougher surface of glass makes applying labels difficult, and we get a lot of rejects. Plastic would be lighter and cheaper to ship too. If plastic is recyclable, more easily labeled, cheaper to ship, and thus more profitable, why do I insist on using glass?

"Ask the environment!" is my refrain. My concern about the

health of the environment is such that avoiding any kind of assault, no matter how slight, is my highest priority. Not even "recyclable" plastic is totally recyclable. To make new plastic you need a measure of virgin plastic, which uses petrochemicals. Glass, on the other hand, is made of sand, which is in abundant supply. If my customers can live with a glass container, I'm going to ship glass. It's better for the environment. Another company might find its Middle Way in recyclable plastic. But recyclable plastic runs counter to our company Mission and identity. Tom's of Maine was founded on its commitment to the environment.

I'm certainly not the only one in the company who feels this way. A few years ago, the manufacturing team was determined to cut back on the company's astronomical water bill. But it wasn't just a matter of money; inspired by the Mission, they were just as eager to figure out if we were wasting water. The team circled up, discussed the problem, and suggested various causes and appropriate solutions. The culprit, they concluded, was the "rinse-down," or cleaning of the manufacturing equipment after every batch of product was made. Their solution: Install water-saving nozzles on the hoses used in the rinse-down. The result: The first water bill was down 15 percent, and by the end of the first year, the water bill—and water consumption—had been reduced by 25 percent!

Usually, though, the Middle Way is not so obvious. Our new media strategy was the result of considerable work—and tension—on the part of the Tom's and McCabe creative teams. But in the end we came up with a classic Middle Way solution. To get the word about Tom's of Maine to more people, we need the power and reach of television. But we also recognize that it's important to inform people not only about our natural products and our story but also about our Mission. In detail. One minute on television does not do that as well as an advertisement in a newspaper or magazine. We intend to do both—use TV to raise the stature of our product to the millions who may never have heard of Tom's of Maine, and use print to give people the details on our company and Mission. For those in the audience eager to talk back, the 800-number will get them a free sample.

COMPETING BY THE MIDDLE WAY

We'd like PBT within five years to be up to 12 percent from the current 7.5 percent, to throw off more cash for investment and aim for that $100 million sales figure. But how can we pull it off? Our working capital is squeezed. The financial shock of the $400,000 deodorant call back—money we could have used to grow—has reverberated for two years. Next year, we're due to invest in more high-speed equipment. The warehouse is bulging with product. But with working capital squeezed so tight, we can't afford to enter the crucial Rocky Mountain region. Worse still, the national economy remains flatter than anyone in Washington wants to admit. Our sales growth in 1993 seems stymied at less than 10 percent—half our average of the past five years. We're behind the $20 million in sales we predicted.

It's not a pretty picture. My management team is now grinding away in the trenches, trying to hold our ground, searching for ways to boost sales in spite of our limited capital and the sluggish economy. With the big companies testing the natural-ingredient and children's toothpaste markets, my managers are worried about getting killed out there on the shelves.

But I'm pumped. My competitive juices are flowing. I'm trying to get my troops out of their foxholes to look at the horizon, to see what lies in the valley beyond. I know that the decisions we make today will affect what we do three years from now. No longer can we take it one step at a time. We have to try to guess what's on the other side of that horizon.

I've told the board that I'm ready to work my tail off to compete. I want to build a brand and a corporate culture that will survive us, a wonderful company that we can hand on to our children and grand-children. To help move toward our goal of $100 million in sales, I want to hire a new head of R&D.

In one-on-one conversations with top executives and board members, everyone has reinforced my sentiment that now is the time to move forward. That the competition has already started to nibble away at our "natural" strategy is clear to everyone. The consensus is that Tom's of Maine has demonstrated how successful a company like ours can be, and we have to follow up with a strategy that seizes every opportunity. There is surprising agreement that a 20 to 25 percent growth curve is required, even if it means raising more money; the board also seems to agree that improving PBT from 7.5 to 15 percent is also crucial.

Ruth Pertilo has been typically astute. She points out that there is an "authenticity" to what Tom's of Maine is about. Our products, she explains, are not just unique; there is also a "specialness" about them that comes from the essence of the company. Procter & Gamble might create a natural brand of toothpaste because it sees a market to exploit; Tom's makes a natural brand because we wouldn't have it any other way.

As a company we have successfully integrated our values. But to continue to succeed, we have to prove that we can also manage—and *compete*—according to our values.

For many people, what I've just said may appear to be a contradiction in terms. How can you compete in business by *values*? Isn't the cutthroat competition of business the exact opposite of managing by values? *Competition* is a dirty word—but not by our definition at Tom's of Maine.

COMPETITION CAN
BE SCARY—AND FUN

I played basketball at Moses Brown, a small all-male boarding school run by the Quakers in Providence, Rhode Island, that, believe me, is no basketball power in New England. But we had a great coach who took a bunch of tall, uncoordinated teenagers like myself, and even short, rugged ones, and turned us into a team. Outclassed man for man by the competition, we still managed to achieve winning seasons. Our coach had supplied us with a few secret weapons: He taught us to try our best and leave it at that. Our long practices and physical training proved to us game after game that we were better than we thought, and by working as a team, we overcame our deficiencies as individuals. We learned that the team was better than self. Then we ran up and down the court, all five of us, grabbing rebounds, hitting the outside man, fast-breaking downcourt to score, and running the other guys off the court. We finished the year league champions.

Sports analogies are probably used too much in business. But like business, sports is about competition; it's literally the name of the game. It is in sports that many of us (including women executives, thanks to equal opportunity efforts in school sports) first experience the joy of competition. I've never forgotten the thrill of being a champion. The recognition from others that "you're good" is an affirmation of something you found out along the way: You're good.

When the word *compete* appeared in a draft of a mission statement for the Moses Brown School (this former basketball player is now on the board), an educator on the board protested. "I'm firmly opposed to that word *compete,* she said. Another educator on the board seconded her displeasure. But the businesspeople on the board disagreed. Both sides could easily agree that we wanted students to learn about themselves and that accepting a challenge is a perfectly legitimate way to gain self-knowledge. But isn't that a form of competition? "Meeting challenges" is not necessarily the bright-lights variety of competition usually identified with sports; nor need it be a desire to dominate another, to crush the other side, as in the Vince Lombardi school of sports. ("Winning isn't everything; it's the only thing" are not the words I want to live by.) But our children have to meet challenges every day in school and in the schoolyard. They have to pass tests, get into college, find a job. They will have to compete.

At Tom's there are reservations about my goal to become the number-one brand among people who care about health, nature, and their communities. "To become the brand of choice was my former employer's goal," pointed out one Tom's executive, who was also one of the most committed to the Mission. "And that goal seemed to be reasoned in terms of the owner's appetite to get rich." I explained that in our case what was at issue was not getting rich but staying in the game. We have to protect our flanks from the competition's counter-assault, and we can best do that by serving our customers and attracting more of them to our products as quickly as possible. Like my high school basketball team, we have to outrun our tougher (and richer) opponents.

What gives competition a bad name is that some people play *only* to win. Every one of us in the business world has dealt with wheelers, dealers, and opportunists. Early in our toothpaste business, Tom's of Maine's five-year monopoly in health food stores was challenged by a shampoo competitor. The trick up its sleeve: It had hired away our plant manager who knew the secrets of the entire Tom's of Maine manufacturing process that we ourselves had designed especially for preservative-free formulations. We were amazed that a Maine native could head off to the West Coast and disclose our secrets to a competitor, but he did. A decade later, however, we still dominate this competition. Even in business, nice guys don't always finish last.

There is one more element of competition that is usually ignored by its detractors: the joy of it. Many of us simply like playing the game. Competition is a way of measuring and testing ourselves. We like the thrill of challenge. We like to play hard against others. It's in our nature. We can't help it, and as long as it doesn't hurt anyone— and better still, if it helps people—then why not meet the challenge? As Chet says,

> In business, you can expect challenges that can make obtaining your goal more fun. You won't always meet every challenge, of course, but you're bound to learn how to do things differently next time or learn to do with what you have. It's the balance that counts.

There's a Middle Way in competition too. At Tom's of Maine we're convinced of that. Indeed, our survival depends on it! As our competitors with their very big guns circle us, we know we have a secret weapon: The Tom's of Maine Mission to manage for profit and for the common good.

THE SCARY PART:
CAN WE SUCCEED?

As I try to make Tom's of Maine a different kind of company, I'm haunted by the specter of Cheneyville. My wife's ancestors, the Cheneys, spent generations building a great American company while nurturing the community around it. Beginning in the nineteenth century, the Cheneys created America's largest and finest silk industry. From wallcovers to fine silk cravats, Cheney silk was the standard of excellence. Company profits created Cheneyville (now Manchester, Connecticut), built its libraries, schools, and theaters. As was the tradition in those days of patriarchy, the Cheney men passed the family tradition of social responsibility to the next generation; the Cheney women nurtured the cultural life of the community.

Then in 1950, America discovered "synthetic fibers." The Cheney silk profits soon vanished, and so did the family's good deeds. The lesson was not lost on me: Tom's would continue to support good causes only so long as it was profitable. But I am not willing to do just anything for profit. I'm also committed to the common good. How can I pursue both goals—and avoid being gobbled up by my competitors?

Can Tom's of Maine really become the brand of choice in personal care for people who care about health, the natural world, and their communities? We're all willing to try. I asked at a similar crossroads five years ago whether my management team was up for such a challenge. I put the question to them in a special meeting. The manager of our oral-care brand countered with his own question: "What if remaining true to our beliefs and attitudes is not an adequate competitive strategy?"

It was a tough question, but it required an honest answer. Tom's of Maine has an obligation to stay in business; it is our moral responsibility to our shareholders and employees to stay alive. I was as candid as I could be: If our strategy to manage for profit and the common good fails, I said, then we have no alternative but to sell our equity to the competitor whom we believe can best offer job security while maintaining our values and while growing the brand.

What other answer was there? The marketplace is unforgiving in how it separates the winners from the losers. Competitors who can spend the equivalent of our almost $20 million total sales on advertising are going to market with nonalcoholic mouthwash, lichen deodorant, baking soda and children's toothpastes—*our products*. Of course, those companies do not have quite the same values we do. But historically, the marketplace doesn't care that you contribute to causes or are active in protecting the environment.

To survive as who we are, with the kind of values we care about, Tom's of Maine has to change the marketplace's perception of the value-oriented business. We have to continue to grow gradually, market by market, region by region; we have to strike a blow at our competitors with an occasional innovative twist—the vegetable-based glycol in our deodorant is a perfect example—to remind the big players that the innovator in the personal-care-products field is still Tom's of Maine.

All the while we have to get our message to the consumers: that we care about what you care about—people and the environment as well as a good product.

We now know that our Mission and beliefs are as important to some consumers as our natural ingredients themselves. The focus groups we've run on the McCabe media campaign proves that even people who've been using the same toothpaste all their lives or who buy what's on sale understand the appeal of Tom's of Maine once they understand *natural* toothpaste and *natural* deodorant in the context of all the other changes they have made in their lives to be healthier and more concerned about the environment. Once we inform these same people that as a company we put our money where our mouth is—that we actually donate part of our profits to groups and causes— they become very excited about Tom's of Maine. That they care, which we've only recently confirmed, comes as a relief, to say the least. It also comes as a great inspiration.

There is a big place out there in the market for even a small company like Tom's of Maine. To compete, however, Tom's of Maine cannot just be another personal-care company. There are too many bigger kids on the block. We have to be a personal-care company that *educates* consumers, that *reforms* the way business is typically done. To do this, we have to put "the whole" of who we are and what we do out there for the consumer to see. Our authentic self is now our most competitive self.

In the past, we pursued a socially responsible business strategy because we deeply believed it was the right thing for a business—a business with a soul—to do. Now we know it's also the most *competitive* thing for Tom's of Maine to do. I can read your mind. "He thinks he can compete," you're wondering, "but where is this guy going to get the money?"

COMPETING AGAINST THE
POWERS THAT BE—BY THE MIDDLE WAY

Merging with a competitor with deep pockets would violate our principle of autonomy. We've opted for family control and waved good-bye to the marketing and media budget that a rich "partner" would bring to the table. Investment bankers won't be much help either; even small regional underwriters sniff at any deal under $15 million. Not only would I not know how to spend that kind of money, but given the current worth of Tom's of Maine anyone who invested $15 million in us would end up owning more of the company than I want to give up. So what's my alternative?

Forget leapfrog. The game I want Tom's of Maine to play is one of stepping from stone to slippery stone, carefully and deftly—all the way to $100 million in sales over several years. Better yet, I'll gamble that we will hop from dry stone to dry stone quickly by power of our new creative advertising campaign, tighter coordination with our retail-store promotional opportunities, and a little luck. The reality may be, in fact, that high, profitable growth of a company that knows itself, knows how to do it, and learns day by day how to do it better, may be a powerful new engine that delivers us to the other side of the stream before we know it. This is a good Middle Way kind of strategy. We'll definitely need new money for media and new markets, such as the Rocky Mountain region. We must get our deodorant on the shelves in our existing toothpaste markets. I think five million dollars will do the trick. I'm confident that the money will come from an increase in profits, from a private investment banker with whom we've worked who shares our commitment to Maine, and if necessary, from individuals who would like to invest in a unique company like Tom's of Maine. That's my *financial* Middle Way.

The Middle Way approach has brought us to the edge of a major breakthrough in the one area that has eluded Tom's of Maine for years: establishing the professional credibility of our toothpaste. The American Dental Association (ADA) seal of approval would increase our sales exponentially overnight! We have been trying to get an ADA endorsement for years. The Tom's of Maine board has reminded us often of the financial benefits of being able to say, "Dentists recommend Tom's of Maine." The official ADA protocol requires testing the product on animals, which we refused to do. Kate actually found a better way—a Middle Way, in fact—by devising a human study with a major university. This took longer and cost more, but it proved the efficacy of the Tom's brand of toothpaste. Nevertheless, the ADA's council on dental therapeutics advised us that our application for its seal of approval could not be approved unless we dropped *natural* from the name of the brand. Apparently, the ADA's definition of *natural* applies only to a product of nature that happens to clean teeth (just as a "natural" sponge soaks up water). That toothpaste is by definition a *man-made* concoction to clean teeth and that one made only from natural ingredients ought to qualify as "natural" seems to elude their sense of logic.

We, however, were not about to yield our claim to being a natural toothpaste. (We certainly aren't an artificial one or one made from artificial ingredients.) We seemed stymied between the either-or of dropping the *natural* from our brand name and having no endorsement—until this winter, when we explored a Middle Way. Tom's of Maine is now in consultation with a special team of dental authorities on periodontal disease and cariogenics. We have decided to forgo the ADA seal of approval and let another scientifically eminent group affirm the professional credibility of Tom's of Maine toothpaste.

THE MIDDLE WAY
REQUIRES COMPETITION

"Aren't we already a commercial success?" one of my top executives asked recently, pointing to our sales figures. "We have a strong customer base; they're loyal and growable. And we've learned to manage for the common good as well as for our own private good."

In his mind that added up to commercial success. It does in my mind too. But that success is not likely to last if we don't achieve one more goal—a defensible consumer franchise. If our competition beats us in the health markets, we've lost our franchise and can no longer call ourselves "the leader with customers who care about natural ingredients." To defend our franchise, we have to stretch ourselves to the limit to be first in our traditional markets. We have to get into new markets and establish our diversity on the shelves. Add in the new deodorants and mouthwashes we've got in the works, plus a totally new product line that I cannot even divulge at the moment, and we should keep the competition off balance while we continue to grow.

The rest is out of our control. All we can do is continue to do what we do best: manage Tom's of Maine creatively, according to the values we believe in, and try to protect our autonomy. The profit, we now know, will be part of the total result.

MANAGING BY THE MIDDLE WAY

Effective managing by the Middle Way depends on you having your own clear understanding of your values and beliefs, your company identity, and your company mission. Because values are personal, every values-driven company will be driven differently. While your Middle Way will be individual to you and your company, however, you need to establish it vis-à-vis some firm objectives. You need to navigate between some firm operating principles and the demands of the marketplace; you need to navigate between managing for profit and for the common good.

1. Reflect on the day-to-day challenges your business faces. Are your suppliers' charges going up? Are sales flat, production costs increasing, the board unhappy? What are the different courses of action you could pursue? To find the Middle Way, you need to determine the most extreme, opposite courses for each situation, short-term and long-term. Then take something from each to determine the Middle Way. Remember, the Middle Way does not mean, necessarily, a balanced solution—you're not taking equally from both sides. It's a *practical* solution that borrows from both courses.

2. The short-term Middle Way may be dramatically different from the long-term. For instance, you may need to cut costs now by using some nonrecyclable materials in order to establish a brand; once it is established, you can use less wasteful packaging. Or you may pay out more in incentives to your employees now in order to reduce overall costs over the next five years. Or you may need to consolidate your operations now in order to expand them later.

3. Finding the Middle Way for long-term goals is not always so obvious. Keep in mind your values as you chart your way into the future marketplace and as you determine how you will compete.

   • To compete effectively, fall back on your strengths.

   • What are your company's and your employees' passion points? Make your strategy and purpose as highly partic-ular as you can.

4. In determining the Middle Way in managing for the natural environment, consider the following:

   • Is the ingredient or material you're using a renewable resource? Have you taken into account the cost of its depletion? Have you factored in the cost of restoring this resource if it's replaceable?

   • In your manufacturing or production process, have you factored in the cost to your community, its health and well-being—the common good—of the waste or pollu-tion you create? Have you thought of the long-term destruction to your own business from future assess-ments or charge-backs by the public for damages to natural resources?

5. There is no "right" Middle Way. You can find your way *between* the shores by keeping *each* in sight.

WORKING FOR

THE PRIVATE AND

THE COMMON GOOD

A month ago, Brian Holland, who coordinates community relations for our marketing department, telephoned City Year, a
service group in Boston, to inform them that Tom's of Maine wanted
to donate a thousand dollars to their work with inner-city children.
There was silence on the other end of the phone, and then a voice
answered, incredulously, "You want to give us money? *You're* calling
us?" I myself have been a volunteer all my life and have served on the
boards of more groups than I care to count. Every one of them shared
the same dilemma: How are we going to raise the money to do the
things we ought to do? If I were sitting at home and suddenly got a

call from some company wondering whether I could use a thousand dollars, I'd drop the phone.

In 1993 Tom's of Maine spent more than $300,000 on public education and community organization sponsorships—absolutely separate from our tithed, donations budget. We now get more than three hundred requests a year for donations. Still, many of the programs and groups we'd like to help don't know about our grants or sponsorships policy. So we've begun shopping around, seeking out groups and organizations whose work is in line with our company Mission. (I won't say we don't get some pleasure from the shock of disbelief when we call out of the blue to offer a group a donation.)

City Year, which has been called "the new urban peace corps," works with some four hundred inner-city kids from kindergarten through fifth grade. We wanted to sponsor a four-day environmental camp that would focus on education about the rain forests and wetlands, as well as environmental issues in the Boston area. Tom's would pay for plants, materials, and a trip to the Rainforest Exhibit at Boston's Franklin Park Zoo, thus enabling city kids who don't really have a chance to connect with nature to do so right in their own backyard.

At Tom's of Maine, we have chosen goodness. But this commitment to goodness is not limited to our good products or their success. Nor is it limited to our good relations with employees and the great strides we've made toward creating a genuine community among the eighty-five employees who now work at Tom's. For us, the measure of goodness is being held accountable to the values and expectations of the community—the common good. Again, it is in line with the Tom's of Maine Mission:

 To be a profitable and successful company, while acting in a socially and environmentally responsible manner.

We have set out to manage for profit *and* for the common good. At the outset, we assumed that our profits would drive our Mission of social responsibility. After all, a company that doesn't make money will not have any to give away. We have recently discovered, however, that the Mission itself attracts customers to our products, increasing our profits—and thus enabling our significant contribution to company good deeds. We have discovered, in fact, that you don't have to sell your soul to make your numbers.

Once confused about my priorities, I am now very clear: The ultimate goal of business is *not* profit. Profit is merely a means toward the ultmate aim of affirming the health and dignity of human beings and their families, affirming aspirations of the community, and affirming the health of the environment—the common good. If our air is polluted, our communities and people polluted, how can our businesses really prosper? What business leaders need to recognize is the awesome power we have to turn our ingenuity and cash flow toward helping others. American companies have to think not only of their private good but the common good. This is what I have discovered on my journey from entrepreneur to divinity student and back again. This is my message—and challenge—to my fellow business leaders:

The world has changed. So must business. We must create a new kind of capitalism—with a heart and a soul.

THE PRIVATE GOOD VERSUS
THE COMMON GOOD

Historically, doing business in our capitalistic system has been about *private* companies pursuing maximum profit within the limits of the law. The business of business has been making money, and the result in America, especially in this century, has been growing affluence for more people and a quantum leap in technological progress. But this progress has had its downside. The Industrial Revolution opened a chasm between the public and the private; the workplace was separated from the home. Rational calculation and utility belonged to business, while values became the province of the home, school, and church. Factories polluted the air and water, and when business and industry fled the cities in the 1960s to maximize profits, so did the middle class. Left behind were a growing number of unemployed as well as an increasingly unemployable "underclass," too many of whom turned to crime to make a living or sought relief from their misery in drug and alcohol addiction.

The pollution of the air and rivers was long passed off as a necessary evil of doing business. But by the late 1980s, even the most intransigent apologists for industrial pollution had to concede that pollution cannot be sanctioned or justified forever; nature, unlike poverty perhaps, has its limits. Polluted rivers eventually die. The destruction of the rain forest spins off environmental injuries to the air and sun and to people thousands of miles away. Scientists have confirmed the damage, forecasting more doom. Nations have agreed to try to reverse the damage. Conserving the environment may be the most powerful force for change in America. Wherever you live, people are trying to do something to help, sustain, and protect the environment.

Is there anyone—or any company—who can argue that the future health of the planet is not in their interest? Are you willing to say to your children or grandchildren that you don't give a damn about the condition of the world you will leave them?

Even private companies have public responsibilities. We all have an interest in the common good.

THE PRIVATE GOOD AND
THE COMMON GOOD COMBINED

Tom's of Maine is in every way a *private company*. Legally, we are a privately held family company. Like any other private company, ours is committed to "incentivism"—we have nothing against paying big salaries and big bonuses to encourage our employees to aspire to big market shares, big growth rates, and other big challenges. We are hardly in business only for the fun of it or for praise. We are motivated by success and its high profits. But at work at the center of our company, which balances our appetite for incentives and profit, is the spirit, the heart, the feeling that no matter how good success and profit may be, no matter how good rational analysis and strategies toward those goals may be, the common good is better.

Truly closed groups, whether families or clubs or businesses or special interest groups determined to function on their own without admitting outside perspectives into their planning, have their own version of what's good. But even the private good of these "private spheres," as Jonathan Edwards called them, is accountable to the values and expectations of the public sphere of good—also known as "the commonweal" (the common wealth) or the common good. Every company has a right to pursue its own private aims, especially profitability; but that private aim must be held accountable to the values common to that free society. Our common good calls more and more for respecting the dignity of all life, human, animals, and the environment.

Let's get honest with one another: I, too, can play the numbers game. The pretax profit of our businesses can vary from 10 to 25 percent. The donations we give to needy groups is no more than *one percent of our sales*—and it connects us to the common good in a big way. Is donating one percent of sales an inconceivable shift in thinking? Customers are telling us in focus groups that they like knowing that the money they're spending helps other people. I know my employees affirm the policy, and I know that the Tom's of Maine owners and directors believe the policy is marginal in cost but huge in impact. In fact, a little does go a long way.

According to Jonathan Edwards, the best of what we are is in our bond to others (once again that Edwardsian refrain: "being is relation"). It is this bond, this spiritual connection, that points us as a company to the common good. As our Statement of Beliefs says,

 We believe that both human beings and nature have inherent worth and deserve our respect.

According to our Mission, Tom's of Maine aims

 to address community concerns, in Maine and around the globe, by devoting a portion of our time, talents, resources to the environment, human needs, the arts, and education.

WHY CARE ABOUT THE
COMMON GOOD?

I've heard CEOs say, "Let Tom's of Maine pursue the common good. I'm in business to make as much dough as I can. In fact, that's my *moral responsibility* to my stockholders. I can't go around giving away ten percent of my profits!"

My counterargument: If you believe in morality, then you really don't have a choice. All of us in business are dependent on more people than our bankers or stockholders. What about your owners, employees, supplies, customers, government, and nature? Whenever there is this kind of interrelation, there will be moral responsibility. It is morally wrong for any boss to humiliate an employee, exploit his work, steal her ideas, pay him unfairly, or harass her sexually. It is no less morally wrong to violate the environment.

Native Americans have a saying, "You cannot sell the land; the land is God's creation." In a sense, the land we own is on loan to us, no matter how many legal deeds we may have. When we pass on, our children will take over; most Americans have finally come to under-stand that if the land (or national debt) our children inherit is catastrophic, they will be right, morally right, to hate us for what we did to them. Spiritually and morally, we all share creation.

MEETING ON THE VILLAGE GREEN

I started my own business with two motives in mind: self-expression, something I quickly discovered was not going to be encouraged at Aetna; and to put a whole different set of values into the marketplace to be tested—*my* values, my wife's values, our fam-ily's values. So we created a special kind of company where from the outset, I now recognize, my private sphere (my desire to make money with a private family company) worked with my public sphere (the values that connected me to my consumers and the community at large—respect for people and nature). Put even more simply, I wanted to acquire *and* to share.

At divinity school, I learned from Martin Buber and Jonathan Edwards that relationships with others, the give-and-take, are not just part of life, they are what makes life—and business—worth doing. I recall standing with Clint, my director of finance, at a Tom's of Maine gathering. He looked around proudly and said, "It just seems so right and it feels so good to be together and to look at what we do and what we are, and to see what we've become." Edwards would have called it beautiful.

What we've become is a company that has managed—not without some difficulty, controversy, and wounded spirits—to recognize that businesses, too, have public spheres—customers, suppliers, community, nature, even the future—that can be combined with their private aims successfully and profitably. This convergence of the private and the common good at Tom's is, as Colleen Myers has pointed out, like the traditional American village green. I'll let Colleen explain what she means:

> When we get together as a company, what we see is not ourselves in our day-to-day roles at Tom's, but ourselves as individuals with families, and as part of a community that is like a village. Standing in the large open space outside our elevator, like a village green, we just mingle as though we were neighbors on our way to church or to the marketplace or whatever. We exchange *human* greetings, which I think is part of what enables us to go back to our jobs without losing that sense of the other as a whole person.

As this goodness flows through the company like an invisible electric current, it is bound to find its way to the outside, to the community beyond the walls. A good company—a company where goodness is appreciated and encouraged—will want to do good for the community. When values enter the workplace and commerce, they begin to blur the separation between private and public in a very good way.

The new company chemist, Pam, who used to work for one of our large competitors, told me recently,

> In my former job, I was in an isolated department. I had no relation to the whole of the company. But the Tom's of Maine Mission Statement helps me feel part of the whole company here. It also helps me look at myself and my own role and see how important it is. I've been changed here by the ethics of the Mission. It has in fact made me examine my own mission in life.

Pam's "outside, personal" life has merged with her professional life. The values she has taken from the Mission have inspired Pam and her husband to be more discerning shoppers, label-readers, more aware of their role in the community.

At Tom's we have discovered that our respect for people and nature has had a ripple effect in the respect we show to our customers and the kinds of organizations to which we give our money. You cannot go out of your way for other people, you cannot be intentional about doing good, without being changed. What has been equally gratifying (and much more surprising) is that our efforts to do good have often produced financial as well as emotional rewards.

"JOIN US"

In 1992 the Boston public television station WGBH asked us for a $400,000 grant to cosponsor a new TV series on the environment, eventually entitled *Earthkeeping*. The producers were not planning the usual gloom-and-doom picture of environmental devastation favored by the press and television. Instead, they had set out to find individuals, communities, and corporations who actually had come up with practical solutions for rolling back environmental decline. The premise of *Earthkeeping*, which was aired over public TV nationwide, was to convert concern for the environment into action, by proving that each one us can really make a difference.

"This is everything we are" was our reaction at Tom's. The head of marketing and I agreed that the company had to be involved. But how to find the dollars? An investment in a public television program would certainly be an investment in the common good. But the year before we had already helped WETA, the Washington, D.C., public television station, underwrite *Making Sense of the Sixties* with a grant of $125,000, which already seemed pushing the envelope. (I repeat, goodness is always accountable—in this case, to the company budget.) In spite of the bite out of the bottom line, the company knows when it has its own peculiar opportunity to be itself. Our decision? "Just do it, and find a way to cover our backside!" we said. We decided to pursue both our private *and* common goods by integrating the $400,000 public television grant with our total marketing plan. The television series, we believed, could become a way to connect to retailers and new customers. The overriding marketing theme was "Join Us"—in building the common good as well as profits.

We worked closely with WGBH in promoting a video contest tied to the series, encouraging the audience to submit videos of their own efforts to reverse environmental disaster. To spread the word about *Earthkeeping,* we packed inserts into our toothpaste cartons alerting customers to the dates the progams would air. The marketing and community life departments informed grassroots environmental groups in New England about the series and the contest, encouraging them, too, to spread the word among their members, volunteers, and newsletters. To generate interest at Tom's of Maine, we held a special Earth Day celebration—the series debuted the evening before Earth Day 1993—where the executive producer of *Earthkeeping* showed an excerpt. We wanted everyone in the company to feel that they, too, were sponsoring this new TV series.

But our major coup—an incredible marketing breakthrough for a small company like Tom's of Maine—was the joint promotion for *Earthkeeping* we did with the CVS/People's drugstore chain, our biggest customers, with eighteen hundred stores on the East Coast. Tom's sent out a direct-mail piece to 200,000 consumers encouraging them to watch the series. We also explained that we were underwriting the series because of our own commitment not only to the environment but to the common good. Again putting our money where our mouth is, we provided consumers in the direct-mail piece with a coupon that saved them a dollar if they bought two Tom's of Maine products—one oral, the other a body-care item. (Encouraging customers to buy more than toothpaste would help us diversify the Tom's of Maine brand.) The coupon was redeemable only at CVS. CVS topped off this extraordinary joint effort by supplementing the shelf display of our brand with special displays of our products at the ends of the aisles (endcap displays, as retailers call them) in all their primary chains and outlets—a historic first for Tom's.

The irony was as big as the promotion: Tom's of Maine had achieved a landmark marketing coup with an idea that had not grown out of our advertising and promotion budget. It was simply a gift that dropped out of the sky because we were trying to serve the common good. Simply by following our instincts to get involved with a good project—*Earthkeeping*—we entered a new kind of partnership with a multimillion-dollar drugstore chain. Through our support for a television series that would educate Americans about how they might personally help the environment, we had achieved the biggest sales opportunity in our twenty-three-year history. Another good result: The head of CVS's corporate donations program began working with Colleen on new ways to increase the sales of both our companies, as well as our shared commitments to the common good.

Goodness begets goodness. We have discovered this time and time again at Tom's of Maine.

Join Them—and They Might
Just End Up Joining You

In the summer of 1991 the community life department got a call from the Rainforest Alliance, a nonprofit educational group that was looking for a small grant to help fund a symposium on biodiversity at Rockefeller University in New York City. The amount of money requested was reasonable, and we were impressed by how much homework the Rainforest Alliance had done on Tom's of Maine. After reading more about the group and the proposed symposium, I was not only eager to contribute, I wanted to attend. In January 1992, Katie Shisler and I went to Rockefeller, where we met scientists from all over the world—ethnobotanists, ethnopharmacists, biochemists—researching the medicinal value of plants. It was a remarkable experience for someone like myself, who had been fascinated by the wonders and possibilities of nature all my life. For only a small grant, I had made connections to scientists and research from around the world.

After learning more about the Rainforest Alliance's efforts to sustain the diversity of the ecosystem of the rain forest and to help native peoples, Tom's of Maine made an additional $100,000 grant spread over three years to help fund four specific projects, three of them in Brazil. While I was at the Earth Summit in Rio in 1992, I decided to pay a visit to our three Brazilian grantees, a child malnutrition project and a clinic for mothers and children in the northeastern state of Ceará, one of the poorest parts of the country.

There the staff had been taught to harvest and grow medicinal plants that they could use to help patients. It was part of the Green Pharmacy Project, which included an original garden of one hundred carefully selected medicinal species and a series of satellite gardens, each located in an area of poverty with the same one hundred medicinal plants. (Imagine an area of green filled with medicinal plants in the middle of Boston's Roxbury neighborhood or the South Bronx.) Tom's of Maine helped fund the research and maintenance of the plants in the main garden, under the supervision of Dr. F. J. Abreau Matos, who is compiling extensive information about the medicinal qualities of local plants from members of the indigenous communities, most of which were breaking apart due to economic and environmental forces beyond their control.

The combination of these ancient remedies and modern medical insights has created some incredible results. Dr. Matos showed us pictures of children thin and wizened from malnutrition; then we saw pictures of these same children three months later, after they had been fed and treated with plants from the local "green pharmacy." Miraculously, their arms were plump, their hair shiny, their wide eyes bright with life and hope.

During this visit, we discovered that Matos's fellow researcher, Dr. Alfrania Craviero, also one of our grantees, was working with plant oils that might be used with other products manufactured around the world. Tom's of Maine has contracted Dr. Craviero to look for applications that might enhance or extend our line of personal-care products. Already we have discovered that lemongrass oil, an extract from a plant that grows in dry soils of Ceará, could substitute for the lichen we now use in our natural deodorant.

None of this would have happened if I had simply written a check to the Rainforest Alliance and left it at that. Our involvement in plant research in Brazil is just more evidence that if you choose to do good, you will find goodness in the most unexpected places.

As gratifying as these successes are, we have not forgotten that doing good begins at home, in the company, in the private sphere. The glitter of international conferences and the adventure of trips into the rain forest have not overwhelmed our commitment to respecting the people who work for Tom's. No company—it's important that I repeat this—can give away money if it doesn't make any. Our employees are the ones who make sure the company keeps growing. But they, too, have to grow, and to help them we have set up a company clearinghouse for classes and training programs.

Training for

the Common Good

We have never thought of ourselves as a school, but the more Colleen and I talked about training needs at Tom's, the more we realized that the company required some kind of internal program for helping employees get more comfortable with the Mission, as well as information and access to programs, consultants, and courses at local colleges and universities that would improve their work skills and career possibilities. Colleen's team has been ingenious about working out combinations of in-house programs and courses available nearby. A smart consumer, she has shopped around for value and thus had success at providing most employees with at least some of the training they thought they needed. When the office staff said they needed training in word processing and computer spreadsheets to be more effective, we put the time and money into that technical training. Community life directed employees eager to improve their business writing skills to a free adult-education class at the local high school. If any employee has to be away from the job for certain training, we work out an arrangement with someone to cover for them.

Educational opportunities have not been limited to job skills. Living the Mission at Tom's of Maine has not been an easy path. Conflicts between people and priorities emerge every day. Mistakes happen. Frustrations mount. How are we to find our way through the thicket of issues and personalities while affirming the dignity of people and nature—and still make a profit? We try to remember that Tom's of Maine is a company of *permissions,* not rules. We have established the Mission, revised it, and continue to find our way in accordance with it, often winging it.

But in conversations with executives and managers we have gleaned some guidelines about how our employees can better live the Mission. These "permissions" are still in the works, but the community life department will be working hard with employees to:

- *Be clear.* Messages and communications in business too often turn into a version of the parlor game Telephone—by the time the information works its way up the hierarchy, it has become hopelessly garbled. We need regular executive meetings and real communications between departments. "Ask the executive team what is going on" should be a regular question. "Ask the President." Rumors or incoherent messages are a waste.

- *Seek goodness.* Relationships with everyone inside and outside the company are central. There is more to business than the bottom line.

- *Have faith.* Many of our challenges are too big for us alone. Have faith that others will help, and trust that life is about more than work. Faith is the source of patience and perseverance.

- *Grasp autonomy*. You are free to be yourself in serving others. How you serve is your gift and your challenge. Autonomy is not doing whatever you want. We are all accountable to someone. But you do have the freedom to bring creativity to your job, or to change the way you do that job, or to find another job that better suits your talents and ambitions.

- *Respect creation*. Human beings are part of nature. Nature is not just something for us to use. The survival of the environment is a global issue—and it should be your issue. There are many specific things we can all do to help.

- *Work together*. Our model of a successful company is not a person sitting alone with a problem. It is a team, or a partnership. We believe that right relations between employees, mutual relations, produce the best results, for the people involved as well as for the company.

Tom's of Maine encourages employees to seek out educational opportunities to improve their lives and personal relationships outside the company. As I write, the community life department has notified employees about "A Healthy Day for Men and Women" at the University of Southern Maine in nearby Portland, a daylong workshop to educate people about health issues for their bodies, minds, and relationships. (Some of the day's offerings: "Family Relationships," "Personal Finances," "Communications Skills," "Learn an Exercise Program.") A month later, a local hospital is giving a three-hour seminar at Tom's called "How to Identify and Effectively Intervene with a Chemically Dependent Employee." An upcoming brown-bag lunch is being planned called "Self-Empowerment: Feeling Good about Yourself and Others," aimed at increasing the self-esteem of people who seem to have a critical inner voice that hinders their personal and professional accomplishments. An invitation has been posted for an annual conference on women in management. We have planned a three-hour workshop to see how we might bring our current methods of evaluating employee performance into line with our commitment to employee creativity, self-discipline, and growth.

Over the past three years, all of us at Tom's have gotten quite an education about ourselves as well as about our new way of doing business. We learn something from every new risk we take. Our Mission has given us all permission to think freely and responsibly about how we can do our jobs and serve the common good. Our employees have become more committed, more passionate, and more motivated. I don't think any increase in sales or profits has caused this. The real reason is that employees have been motivated—in some cases, impassioned—by the permission to offer up an idea, to go out and serve the public, and to be more affirming toward one another on the job. We have allowed ourselves to change as competitors and, more important, as human beings.

Tom's of Maine has witnessed a genuine change in the spirit of the company—we have found our soul.

THE COURAGE TO CARE

The ultimate result of a business with a soul is, I believe, a new kind of capitalism, a way of doing business that can analyze and strategize—but always with an eye on the common good. Once you taste this new way of doing business, once you find out how wonderful it is to manage for profit and the common good, you will want more. Goodness begets goodness. It begins first inside your company, with executives and employees respecting each other as human beings and not as anonymous job categories; then this current of goodness charges both your customers and your vendors. It's a new spirit that's not just about serving the consumer for fear she will go elsewhere; it's understanding how you stand in relation to that consumer, person to person, and renaming that customer or vendor a friend. I call it "Common Good Capitalism."

Back in 1986, when I retreated into divinity school and away from some traditional business practices, I made the acquaintance of great thinkers, perceptive teachers, and intelligent, caring fellow students, male and female, who reaffirmed my entrepreneurial intuitions. I discovered that there is an alternative to traditional capitalism. I realized that diversity is not necessarily disorder but is a value; that goodness is not only a beautiful sunset but an invisible energy that, when harnessed, can bring people together. I learned that even a private family business is interdependent on all sorts of other people and organizations, and that our private goods must be accountable to the public good.

Between 1986 and 1991, I stepped back from my day-to-day work life and restored my spirit. Still, it has taken me several more years to transform Tom's of Maine into a new kind of company and to build up my own courage in managing for profit and for the common good. Before divinity school I assumed the professional managers I had hired to grow my business knew what they were doing. Even after Harvard, I was still too timid to tell Ed McCabe that I was concerned that the "Simple Wisdom" campaign was not the way to go. No longer. My shyness about the power of managing for the common good is long gone.

I have too much evidence of the success of this new kind of capitalism. Ironically, I even have the numbers to prove that people are buying our products not just because they prefer natural brands but because they prefer turning over their money to a company that will put some of it to good use. We have multiplied our desirability to our retailers. Not only can Tom's of Maine make more money for them per tube of toothpaste than our competitors, we are beginning to entrance them with our new way of commerce.

Tom's of Maine is a living, breathing—and *profiting*—proof that a business enterprise can be good for the earth, good for society, good for its employees, and good for its shareholders. Not even the most rational utilitarian capitalist can ignore the facts and figures of our success. The big companies have been knocking on our door.

MY VISION OF THE FUTURE

Although our corporate suitors all assured us that they would not want to change Tom's of Maine, my response has been the same: My family will continue to control the company. We need our autonomy to keep calling our own shots. Family control gives us the chance to be a new model of a successful business, an inspiration to other corporations who also want to change the face of American business.

In my judgment, something profound is happening in our society. Tens of thousands of people have changed their lives; they eat better, exercise more, and care more about what's in the products they put in and on their bodies. President Bill Clinton was elected on the promise of "change"; polls show that most people do believe that the world is in an environmental crisis; Vice President Al Gore is a respected environmentalist, as are the secretary of the interior and the head of the Environmental Protection Agency. A concern for the common good seems to be building out there, a concern for the common good that is more often understood as common sense.

A few weeks ago, Kate and I received the Environmental Leadership award from the New England Environmental Network. The guest speaker was Secretary of the Interior Bruce Babbitt. The auditorium was filled with about four hundred people, most of them environmental activists, people who devote their lives to changing the government's attitudes toward the environment so that the government can change business's environmental practices. Then there was this award to a small company that has focused on environmental concerns for more than twenty years.

Kate and I were invited to the stage—and then, pandemonium! People clapped and clapped. Their genuine appreciation for what we are doing was so enthusiastic, it was almost embarrassing. *Almost.* We were actually thrilled. These were people who are not big fans of American business. But they applauded our efforts because they saw the connection between us and them, the relation. They welcomed someone new on their village green—a business. It was a moment of deep emotion for us as well as for the audience. It confirmed for me once again that I don't need Nielsen research to tell me that we've got a good idea. This kind of affirmation is what empowers us and inspires us to go on.

I care about America. It's my home, my clan, my identity. I would like those of us in business to own up to our beliefs—that we care about freedom, not freedom to raid nature, but freedom with responsibility and a society of respect for nature, the people, and the creative power of our businesses. All this is inherent in the American cultural identity. We just need to validate it in our own individual circles of influence—that we believe in the value of people, nature, and business and aspire to a new way of being in relation to all three.

We are still the pioneers of the New World. But today's frontier is not the West; it is the even vaster domain of the inner spirit in each of us. In that wide-open interior there is plenty of room to roam, to learn how to link personal aspirations with social consciousness, and to grow.

Kate, long the model for how much women can bring to our circle, has recently given us another model to think about. For the past few years Kate's personal aspirations have been moving away from Tom's of Maine. Taking a cue from the company's success at getting its beliefs and Mission down on paper, Kate had developed a personal statement of beliefs and mission. She has written to her colleagues at Tom's about her own recent journey and plans:

> I believe that life is a journey and that as we grow and change, our understanding of true work changes. . . . I am an artist in everything I do, whether it is cooking, walking, painting, researching, writing, speaking, playing tennis, working in groups, skiing, reading, arranging flowers.

Kate knows herself better after twenty-seven years of marriage, parenting, and growing a business. The garment of the co-entrepreneur no longer fits her; she is looking for a more fitting garment for the person she is becoming. In all, she has been the artist. She will wear that new garment in her work more intentionally. She came to help me in this enterprise, and as a reward, she found herself. Giving seems to work that way.

I, too, have found myself. My whole career has been breaking away from certain constraints—the expectations of the corporate world, of my father, of my young managers. But my new-found autonomy became truly satisfying only when I recognized, through my divinity school studies, that my freedom from certain duties leaves me free to help others. My main goal in life has become perfecting this *freedom to serve* my employees, my customers, my community, and the natural environment that houses and nurtures us all. The Hindus call it *moksa*—a personal mastery of caring less for material things and more for others. *Moksa,* as I see it, is a passionate feeling about who you are and honoring yourself in service to others. It is a freedom to be yourself and also to realize that an inseparable part of you is your desire to serve others. I began as a selfish entrepreneur. Now I would like to become an entrepreneur committed to others.

But I remain a competitor. I still love the game of business, the struggle, the winning. I used to think that the combination of my competitive spirit and my Christian urge to do good would push me into politics. But in the past few years I have realized that I can have a bigger impact on changing things as a successful businessman. And I have more time to work at it. (As CEO of a family-controlled company, I'm not up for re-election every two or four years.) Better still, I have helped create a company and a vision of doing business that can continue after I'm gone.

But while I'm still here, I want my true work to be not just the job of entrepreneur or promoting the Tom's of Maine brand. My task is also to integrate my care for people and my love of the earth with my addiction to competition. The burden of making Tom's of Maine a commercial success requires extraordinary concentration, and I care about what our customers get from us. But the risks that I am accustomed to taking lie beyond just developing brands and assuring a healthy return on investment. I still intend to lead Tom's of Maine, but the entrepreneur in me never seems to stop looking for something new over the horizon.

The valley beyond that I'm now beginning to see more clearly is a new way of combining the aspirations of a free society with the investors and employees of our commercial enterprises.

I know that we—the business community—can change our traditional business culture. The mind will calculate forever, but the heart will eventually give in. We need to help each other. Whatever our differences, our strength is in affirming our identity and joining together to solve our common problems and aspiring to our common aims—to rebuild our community life, to clean up our local waters and air, to reach out to our needy neighbors, to re-seed the village green.

For those of you who feel the same tug, I have a place in Kennebunk, Maine, called Partners for the Common Good. We are private and commercial businesses as well as nonprofit groups working on common causes. We share the same values, work together in different circles, and solve the particular problems of the village green. Informally connected, we ask questions and share stories about how to integrate the common good into our particular businesses. Then we inspire each other to action.

You may not need our help. You may want to venture out on your own, working with other businesses to bring about changes in your own workplaces, your communities, your environment. Change begins within each of us. To get started, you just need encouragement and assistance.

I, for one, encourage you. I've made that change, thanks to all the good people and good spirits I'm connected with. I speculated that a new way was possible, I tried it, and I've been changed by it.

Managing for profit and for the common good—it works.

BIBLIOGRAPHY

Agee, James, and Walker Evans. *Let Us Now Praise Famous Men*. Boston: Houghton Mifflin Company, 1969.

Badaracco, Joseph L., Jr., and Richard R. Ellsworth. *Leadership and the Quest for Integrity*. Boston: Harvard Business School Press, 1989.

Buber, Martin. *I and Thou*, trans. Ronald Gregor Smith. 2nd ed. New York: Macmillan Publishing Company, 1987.

Cassirer, Ernst. *Language and Myth*, trans. Susanne K. Langer. New York: Dover Publications, 1953.

Coleridge, Samuel Taylor. *Biographia Literaria*, ed. George Watson. London: J. M. Dent. Reprinted 1984.

Conze, Edward. *The Perfection of Wisdom in Eight Thousand Lines and Its Verse Summary*, trans. 3rd printing. San Francisco: Four Seasons Foundation, 1983.

Conze, Edward. *Buddhism: Its Essence and Development*. New York: Harper & Row, 1975.

Cooey, Paula M. *Jonathan Edwards on Nature and Destiny: A Systematic Analysis*. Studies in American Religion, vol. 16. New York: The Edwin Mullen Press, 1985.

Dyck, Arthur J. *On Human Care: An Introduction to Ethics*. Nashville: Abingdon, 1977.

Edwards, Jonathan. *The Philosophy of Jonathan Edwards from His Private Notebooks*, ed. Harvey G. Townsend. Westport, CT: Greenwood Press, 1972.

Edwards, Jonathan. *The Works of Jonathan Edwards*, vol. 8, *Ethical Writings*, ed. Paul Ramsey. New Haven: Yale University Press, 1989.

Edwards, Jonathan. *Religious Affections*, ed. John E. Smith. New Haven: Yale University Press, 1959.

Edwards, Jonathan. *Scientific and Philosophical Writings, The Works of Jonathan*

Edwards, vol. 6, ed. Wallace E. Anderson. New Haven: Yale University Press, 1980.

Eliade, Mircea. *Cosmos and History: The Myth of the Eternal Return,* trans. Willard R. Trask. New York: Harper & Row, 1959.

Freeman, R. Edward, and Daniel R. Gilbert, Jr. *Corporate Strategy and the Search for Ethics.* Englewood Cliffs, NJ: Prentice-Hall, 1988.

Hyde, Lewis. *The Gift: Imagination and the Erotic Life of Property.* New York: Vintage Books, 1983.

Kant, Immanuel. *On History,* trans. and ed. Lewis White Beck, Robert E. Anchor, and Emil L. Fackenheim. 1st ed., 18th printing. New York: Macmillan, 1989.

Kant, Immanuel. *Critique of Practical Reason,* trans. Lewis White Beck. 19th printing. New York: Macmillan, 1985.

Kumarajiva. *Scripture of the Lotus Blossom of the Fine Dharma (The Lotus Sutra),* trans. Leon Hurvitz. New York: Columbia University, 1976.

LaBier, Douglas. *Modern Madness: The Hidden Link Between Work and Emotional Conflict.* New York: Simon & Schuster, 1989.

Lindbeck, George A. *The Nature of Doctrine: Religion and Theology in a Postliberal Age.* Philadelphia: The Westminster Press, 1984.

Miller, Perry. *Jonathan Edwards.* Amherst: University of Massachusetts Press, 1981.

Nash, Laura. *Good Intentions Aside: A Manager's Guide to Resolving Ethical Problems.* Boston: Harvard Business School, 1990.

Potter, Karl H. *Presuppositions of India's Philosophies.* Westport, CT: Greenwood Press, 1976.

Schon, Donald A. *The Reflective Practitioner: How Professionals Think in Action.* New York: Basic Books, 1983.

Thurman, Robert A. F. *The Holy Teaching of Vimalakirti: A Mahayana Scripture,* trans. 5th printing. University Park: Pennsylvania State University Press, 1988.

Van Buitenen, J.A.B. *The Bhagavadgita in the Mahabharata,* bilingual edition, trans. and ed. Chicago: University of Chicago Press, 1981.

Welch, Holmes. *Taoism: The Parting of the Way,* rev. ed. Boston: Beacon Press, 1966.

ACKNOWLEDGMENTS

I am particularly grateful to my executive team for their patience during my absence (for writing days), their energy and skill in advancing the business, and for their faith in me. To Chet Homer, Colleen Myers, Kate Chappell, Katie Shisler, Lane Nielsen, Gary Rittershaus, and Clint Marshall, thank you. Likewise, I thank Joan Matthews, my faithful secretary, who maintained equanimity and organization in the chaos of my writing a book, managing a business, and connecting with family members. I am grateful to Blaine Tewksbury, our chemist for eighteen years, from whom I learned as much ethics as chemistry. Your original recipes gave the company a model of creativity. I am incomplete without the insight, guidance, and critical eye of my board of directors and legal counsel. In particular, I thank Mr. Scribner for his unwavering support of Kate's and my enterprise, for his wise counsel and his special care. I have learned from him how to combine shrewdness, kindness, and patience. To my peers and kindred spirits, Dick Spencer, Pam Plumb, Anne Osborn, and to my father-in-law, George Cheney, Jr., thank you for giving us the start and our first years of business. We have lived up to *our* values in business. John Rockwell and Colin Blaydon have successfully helped us transform Tom's of Maine from just another specialty business to a unique, special business leaving a mark on our culture. Thank you for your business wisdom and moral sensitivity. To Pearl Rutledge, thank you for caring for Kate and me in business, for helping our managers through moments of conflict, and for wisdom in directors' meetings. To Bill Schweitzer, my classmate and fraternity brother, thank you for keeping our relationship on an honest, level playing field. I am still your admiring pledge. To Ruth Purtilo, I thank you for asking whether I would publish my term paper for you, my teacher, on "Freedom in Service." It became this book. To Father Phil Allen, I thank you for your willingness to be with us. Your listening helps us understand ourselves.

For help in writing this book, I acknowledge Missy Daniel for her enthusiasm and guidance in the early stages. But I especially acknowledge the miracle worker of this team, Edward Tivnan, who captured my voice and understood my vision in helping to write this book. Your insight, energy, and skill contributed immensely to this project. To Jim Levine, my agent and co-creative director of this book, I especially thank you for your passion, commitment, and eleventh-hour rescue missions to see it to completion. You are a special partner.

To my partners at Bantam, I want to thank my editor, Leslie Meredith, for knowing the importance of this book, for inspiring her colleagues to "claim" it, and for her constructive direction throughout the writing development. To Barb Burg, director of publicity, thank you for your extraordinary excitement for this project. Most significantly, I thank Irwyn Applebaum, president of Bantam Books, for making the success of this book a personal mission.

Among my professors at Harvard, I have Dick Niebuhr to thank in particular. His inspiring curricula design, respect for the mind of the student, and personal interest in my journey prepared me for informed moral leadership. To David Eckel, I thank you for our renewed friendship—this time as student and teacher of Hinduism, Buddhism, and Taoism. Your time with me was a wonderful gift. To Ron Thiemann, Mark Edwards, Ted Hiebert, Arthur Dyck, Helmut Koester, and Elisabeth Schüssler-Fiorenza, thank you for the time each of you spent helping me unravel the mystery of my ministry.

Additional acknowledgment goes to Frances Hancock, my classmate and co-theologian. Your encouragement and faith-in-action helped me affirm that our mission at Tom's was possible. Thank you for your caring. Thanks to Dana Mitchell, a Penobscot, who has taught me more about relations with people, the spirit, and the land; and to my friends George Wiltshire, Bill Allaire, and David Beronä, who helped me keep the challenge of this project focused on today.

Last, I want to thank all the people at my company, Tom's of Maine, whose faith in me has enabled us all to grow more and more toward a just way of serving customers, each other, our community, our natural world, our owners, and future generation. You are a very special community of spirits.

Every story has its audience. Our audience is consumers who seek natural, healthy products in their lifestyle. I thank Paul Hawken for opening that door of opportunity. His creative collaboration and guidance in our first Tom's products were a special gift. I will always value his imagination and friendship.

TOM CHAPPELL founded Tom's of Maine with his wife, Kate, in 1970. Since that time he has dedicated himself to creating a company that produces innovative, healthful products in a caring and creative environment. In 1991, Tom received CNBC-TV's Entrepreneur of the Year award, along with Anita Roddick of the Body Shop; in 1992, both Tom and Kate were selected as the Small Business People of the Year for the state of Maine. In 1993, Tom was honored with the New England Environmental Leadership Award and, with Kate, the Governor's Award of Business Excellence. Tom's of Maine, in addition to creating extremely successful personal-care products like the famed toothpaste, is known for its commitment to nature, to community, and to its employees. Tom's of Maine gives away ten percent of its pretax profits to charity and worthy causes. The company's employees receive unusual benefits such as childcare subsidies and time off to volunteer within the community. The company is guided by a Statement of Beliefs that ends with this striking summation: "We believe our company can be financially successful while behaving in a socially responsible and environmentally sensitive manner."